zen

AT WORK

To Peter—
To Friendship—
To Dharma

[signature]

August
1997

zen

AT WORK

LES KAYE

CROWN TRADE PAPERBACKS
NEW YORK

Published by Crown Trade Paperbacks, 201 East 50th Street, New
York, New York 10022. Member of the Crown Publishing Group.

First paperback edition printed in 1996.

Random House, Inc. New York, Toronto, London, Sydney,
Auckland

http: //www. randomhouse.com/

CROWN TRADE PAPERBACKS and colophon are trademarks of
Crown Publishers, Inc.

Printed in the United States of America

Design by Bonni Leon-Berman

Library of Congress Cataloging-in-Publication Data

Les Kaye.
    Zen at work/Les Kaye.
        p. cm.
        1. Religious life—Zen Buddhism. I. Title.
    BQ9286.L46   1997
    294.3´44—dc20   96-9911
                                                     CIP

ISBN 0-517-88620-0

10 9 8 7 6 5 4 3 2 1

First Paperback Edition

To my mother-in-law,
Katherine Bandelier of Stillwater, Oklahoma,
who has shown for ninety-six years that equanimity,
rather than excitement, is the source of happiness.

contents

acknowledgments

It would not have been possible to create this book without the unselfish support and encouragement of my friends and family.

I am grateful to Cate Hunter for providing the necessary "jump start." Liz Statmore, having eagerly offered to take on the questionable distinction of reading the tentative, incomplete first drafts, never lost her enthusiasm for pointing out good features and making creative suggestions for improving the writing and the structure. Without hesitation, Misha Merrill immersed herself in the long, formidable task of transcribing and editing lectures, and making certain that nothing got lost or distorted in the translation. Authors John Hubner and Jill Wolfson generously took time from their young family and their own challenging work to encourage and show me how to crystallize experience in story. Scott Lowe and my son, David, through their love of writing and literature, gave insightful suggestions for enhancing the clarity and accuracy of what I was trying to say. My daughter Margaret's passion for exploring, living, and reporting the fundamental nature of humanity provided countless joyous opportunities for sharing observations and for clarifying my own understanding. I am fortunate to have had the guidance of Adrienne Ingrum of Crown Publishing, my creative editor and literary trail boss, who kept the strays in line and the herd moving in the right direction. Finally, my wife, Mary, with her consistent common sense, patience, and generosity of spirit, provided the perfect sounding board for my ideas, feelings, and recollection of our journey together.

foreword

Forty years ago, when Zen Buddhism was entering my life in something of the way Les Kaye here describes it entering his, the number of good books on the subject could be counted on the fingers of one hand. Today there are perhaps five times that number. Why, then, another?

One reason is because the Dharma/Truth is infinite. No finite number of books can exhaust it, but the present book meets a specific need. By entering America in this century, Buddhism has resumed the eastward march that took it first to China, then to Korea and Japan. But its present step differs from those earlier ones in bringing it not just to a new place but to a new time: modernity. This poses a greater challenge than the previous migrations did, and the question is whether Buddhism can live up to it.

This book is like a wet finger held to the wind on that question, for the receiving station Les Kaye's life offered Zen was not simply the modern world. It was that world at its cutting edge, as represented by Silicon Valley, the high-tech, fast-lane capital of the computer world that has become something of a metaphor for the future. In a way, Silicon Valley is "the future in microcosm," as we used to say haughtily of MIT during the years I was there. Systems analysis and the product development laboratories of IBM are about as far from Dogen's thirteenth-century zendo as one can conceivably get. The two worlds are polar opposites. Computer chips betoken the future, whereas silent sitting looks not to the past but to an even greater contrast—timelessness. And while technology seeks to improve life by altering its circumstances, Buddhism works on how to *relate* to one's circumstances, whatever they are.

Can these two worlds mix? Not only that they can but how they can is the message of this book. Drawing on his thirty years of Zen study and practice—years that led to his present position as

teacher and spiritual leader at the Zen Meditation Center, known
as Kannon Do (Place of Compassion), in Mountain View, California—Kaye includes the basic teachings of Zen in his pages. (I
was particularly struck by his account of *anicca*, the doctrine of
impermanence and the life consequences that follow from understanding that doctrine.) But the distinctive feature of his book is
the way he lards his expositions of Zen with graphic accounts of
problems encountered in his nine-to-five IBM job, which paralleled his Zen practice, and how he used his Zen to cope with those
problems. The result is a book that should put to rest permanently
the stereotype that meditation belongs with loincloths and caves
in the Himalayas, or in the West with social dropouts in tie-dyed
T-shirts.

One substantive point before I let Kaye speak for himself: Les
Kaye is so uncompromisingly faithful to his Soto Zen tradition in
insisting that meditation must be cut free from expectations that
the reader may be confused by the point. For if nothing can be expected from meditation, why embark on it?

It is true that there would be no reason to enter Zen practice if
there were not the hope—which is a kind of expectation—that it
would in the long run change one's life for the better. After all,
the Buddha himself said, "I teach but one thing: pain and the ces-
sation of pain." But once we have undertaken Zen training, every
further expectation is counterproductive. Expectations will continue to arise, of course; especially at the start, they will erupt. But
one should dispatch them as quickly as possible, for they are the
siren songs, diverting one from the task at hand. To go back to a
point I made earlier, Zen's objective is not to envision and work
for changes in one's circumstances. It is to advance to the point
where every circumstance, whatever its character, can be related
to creatively.

The Perfect Way knows no difficulties,
Except that it refuses to make preferences.

Only when freed from hate and love
Does it reveal itself fully without disguise.
A hair's breadth difference,
And heaven and hell are set apart.

SENG TS'AN, "On Believing in Mind"

If the reader supposes that this means we should never try to change the circumstances we find ourselves in, that is not the case. And if it appears that in saying this I have solved the first conundrum by introducing a second, I plead guilty and urge the reader to keep reading to discover its solution.

I do not think any reader will be disappointed, for this is a rewarding book. With palms together in *gassho*, I bow to Les Kaye respectfully.

HUSTON SMITH
Berkeley, California

preface

[My] Supernatural power and marvelous activity—
Drawing water and carrying firewood.[1]

When you walk by the plate-glass window of a bank, a
bar, or a department store, you may catch a glimpse of something
out of the corner of your eye. You turn toward the glass to see what
it is. For a brief moment, you look at something hauntingly familiar but cannot name it. Then, the flood of recognition pours in.

That's the way it was for me when I first read Layman P'ang's
concise, unceremonious vision of life, stirred by a sense of something that I once knew but had long forgotten. With these few
words, my drowsy awareness awoke to what now seems an obvious
truth, that even our most mundane activities express life's inherent spiritual nature.

Despite the familiar feeling it evoked, the precise poetry also
struck a radical note by proclaiming that everyday human tasks—
not prayer, chanting, asceticism, and other traditional forms of
religious practice—are the expressions of spirituality. Like a per-
sistent mirror held up to my mind, it challenged me to question
my habitual way of thinking, to try to understand why I had forgotten something that I had always known. Why did I make distinctions between life's activities, determining that some were
"spiritual" and others "merely ordinary"? Who decides that carrying a bucket of water is a lesser miracle than curing illness, or-
biting the moon, or even creating life itself? Exploring these
questions, I came to understand that even if I could justifiably
fault society and culture for partly creating such judgments, my
own mind joined the conspiracy, convincing itself that it must
persist in this kind of discrimination in order to keep things in
their places in a rational world.

The first time I heard about Zen, I imagined an exotic world, far
from the noisy atmosphere of everyday life, hidden in ancient

temples obscured by incense, smoke, and Oriental mysticism. My fantasy evaporated soon after I actually started Zen practice, as I became aware that its fundamental qualities are not restricted to mysterious meditation halls but are expressed everywhere, in every ordinary activity. I discovered that embracing Zen emotionally and intellectually was just a small, first step toward understanding the truth of my life. I learned that actual Zen practice is fundamental and that Zen is not limited to sitting on a meditation cushion, reading Buddhist books, listening to lectures, and attending occasional meditation retreats. I came to appreciate how Layman P'ang's brief, modest lines, and the sanctity that they express, dramatically reveal the spirituality of daily life.

I was not interested when my friend Cate—entrepreneur, former Madison Avenue account executive, Tibetan Buddhist—first suggested that I write about my "dual careers" as a technical professional in the corporate world and as a Zen priest. My only interest was to make it possible for others to explore Buddhism and Zen by helping to provide an accessible, supportive environment for practice. I had been given such an opportunity many years earlier, when I stumbled onto a suburban meditation hall. Whatever I have discovered since then has come from actual Zen practice, not from books about it. My main concern, I told Cate, was to take care of our present meditation center and help it continue.

But she persisted. This was her argument: "When you started practice in the midsixties, there were only a few hundred Zen students, mostly in San Francisco, New York, and LA. Today there are thousands all over the country. Back then, most people saw Zen as part of the counterculture. It was kind of a romantic notion. Things have changed. Zen practice is not on the fringes anymore. Zen people today have careers and families. They are all wrestling with the same question you had: How do I express spiritual practice in everyday life?

"You've been working on that one for over twenty-five years. You stayed fully active in the competitive business world while you became more and more involved in Zen practice. Has anybody else done what you've done? Are there any other Zen priests in IBM? Do you know of any other corporate managers who have gone off to monasteries for months at a time and then returned to their jobs? You should share your experience with other people who are searching, just like you searched. You say you want to encourage people to practice? Your story will encourage them."

Her enthusiasm and her reasoning were compelling. But I was reluctant to write a book that might be seen as a how-to manual, a set of instructions for "using" Zen, as if it were one of the many high-tech products that we increasingly invite into our lives. I argued that spirituality cannot be explained because it is not a "thing" to be used. However, several weeks later something happened that made me change my mind.

I received a call from a woman who wanted to talk about meditation. She sounded frustrated.

"Meditation doesn't work," she said. "I've read ten books on meditation and nothing happens."

"Have you actually tried meditation?" I asked.

"No, I haven't."

"Why not?"

"It feels funny; it's embarrassing."

"You mean you feel self-conscious?"

"Yes, I do."

I explained that books about meditation would have very little value for her unless she became actively involved in the practice. I encouraged her to try meditation, beginning in a small way in the privacy of her own home. I offered to help her get started.

This story illustrates that, in learning about anything in life, there is no adequate substitute for actually doing the work, that we have to proceed despite the unfamiliarity of the subject or how we may feel about protecting our self-images. I never heard from this woman again. I'm not sure that she was bold enough to take the first step.

This episode, reinforced by Cate's persistence, helped me realize that the older generation has a responsibility to encourage the next one in any way it can. Sharing our stories is one of those ways. Thirty years have passed since I started Zen practice. I was part of that first generation that eagerly welcomed the teachings and the teachers of the Asian Buddhist meditation traditions. Now there is a new generation exploring Japanese, Chinese, Tibetan, Korean, and Southeast Asian practices, learning how to adapt them to the traditions and culture of this country.

So I have gathered together recollections of my spiritual inclinations, my adventures in exploring Zen practice, and the questions, discoveries, and reflections that have tumbled out of my effort to continue practice in the activities of everyday living. Some provided excitement, humor, and delight; others produced rude, sometimes painful, awakenings. All have been meaningful opportunities for discovery. Here they are as a story passed from one generation to the next.

This book is not only about Zen and work. It is about the expression of spiritual practice at several levels: in the inner life of the individual, in the workplace, and in the entire spectrum of the everyday world. It is not intended to provide specific techniques for solving problems on the job or anywhere else. No book can do that, because that is not the job of spiritual practice. Practice prepares us to respond in a confident, caring way to whatever comes up in life, without creating additional difficulties or needless suffering. Although past experiences naturally guide us, no two situations in life are exactly alike. Each has to be seen with fresh eyes so that we do not blindly cling to words or actions that may have worked in the past but that may not be appropriate in present circumstances.

There are some differences among the several contemplative practices of Buddhism, but essentially they are all practices of mindfulness, of being awake to the reality of what's happening in the present moment. Their common theme is: "Don't worry too much about what you will do when difficulty arises. Continue self-less practice and you will naturally know how to take care of things when the time comes." This doesn't mean that they advocate altogether giving up the use of proven methods and appropriate technologies to solve problems. It only means that the basic attitude or worldview that results from spiritual practice should precede the use of problem-solving techniques.

introduction

In 1961, a young man, recently employed as an engineer at IBM in its heyday, attended a party at the home of a friend. Perusing the bookshelves of his hostess, he discovered a book that was to change his life and, therefore, those of many others over the next twenty-five years. The man was Les Kaye; the book was *The Way of Zen* by Alan Watts.

I don't know what struck him in particular, but the elegant, thoughtful words of Alan Watts must have entered his heart and mind in a deep and familiar way, in what Zen students often describe as a feeling of "coming home." Not long after, Les found his way to the fledgling San Francisco Zen Center and his first teacher, Zen Master Shunryu Suzuki, known as "roshi." Les was profoundly affected by Suzuki-roshi and his teachings, and within five years he was a Zen monk, practicing with a small group in Los Altos, California, where Suzuki-roshi came to speak once a week. Now this might not seem so odd considering the times. Plenty of people in the San Francisco area were doing some pretty exotic things during the sixties and early seventies; Zen practice was just one of the items on the menu. It was not at all unusual for young people to show up on Suzuki-roshi's doorstep with bare, dirty feet and a slightly drugged look around their eyes demanding to know about this "Zen thing." But imagine, if you can, a neatly dressed IBM manager sitting in the midst of all this craziness, someone who continued to have an ordinary home life and drive to work every day, nine to five—that was something else indeed.

While many Zen students dropped out of corporate life and conventional lifestyles to immerse themselves in meditation, Les continued to honor the commitments he'd made before discovering the practice: raising and supporting his family, and being engaged in society. Rather than separating his spiritual life from his everyday, ordinary existence, he worked diligently to find the spiritual *in* his everyday life, to find Zen practice in whatever was in front of him. Some Zen students ridiculed Les for "copping out" by continuing to work in the corporate world and insisted that this was proof that he was not really serious about Zen practice. In retrospect, however, it appears that Les chose a valid, albeit difficult path, which many of his peers now embrace but on which he traveled alone for years.

Now, with thirty years of practice and perspective, he has finally written about his experience in *Zen at Work*. Many people may be surprised to find those two words in the same title; what could a spiritual practice have to do with something as mundane and practical as work? But that is exactly Les's point: Zen is completely ordinary and is to be found and practiced in our everyday work and activities. Making coffee, brushing our teeth, driving the freeway, changing the baby's diaper—the list of everyday opportunities for practice is endless and joyous, as long as we don't try to make some distinction between sacred and profane activities, or between what we like and what we don't like. In *Zen at Work*, Les offers his own experience as proof that these kinds of distinctions exist only in our own small minds, that the truth of life lies in its inherent seamlessness where work, play, and spiritual practice are all threads in a single tapestry.

With Suzuki-roshi's encouragement, Les practiced Zen meditation and continued to work at IBM. By choosing to practice in the middle of the corporate world, Les discovered for himself why basic Buddhism gives Right Livelihood the same weight and importance as Right Meditation in its Eightfold Path. The spiritual functions of Right Livelihood—to utilize and develop one's abilities, to experience the dropping away of ego when joining with others in common tasks, and to build character—are not often manifested in Western society, where work is frequently seen as a kind of "necessary evil" that must be performed in order to afford the luxury of leisure or spiritual practice. The Buddhist view, by contrast, is that work and leisure are merely two sides of the same coin, and that the coin itself is the total expression of spiritual life.

Les experienced this firsthand as he immersed himself in "work practice" at IBM while continuing daily meditation. Hours spent on the cushion clarifying his understanding, developing equanimity, and experiencing the fundamental interconnectedness of all beings were tested and refined on a daily basis behind a desk with whatever and whomever was in front of him, in a place where few others brought the same point of view.

Out of his experience of Zen and work practice, Les created and nurtured Kannon Do Zen Center in Mountain View, California. As a nonresidential center with a flexible schedule of daily meditation and a geographically accessible location, Kannon Do enables students to participate in the practice as much as their personal responsibilities allow. At the same time, Les strongly encourages students to find their practice right in the midst of family and work commitments. Kannon Do Zen Center exists today as a sanctuary where daily life is honored as the very heart of Zen practice and where it is understood that mindfulness and compassion can be practiced wherever we find ourselves. Les, as its teacher, provides an example that such a life is possible.

In his book *Zen Mind, Beginner's Mind*, Suzuki-roshi said:

> Here in America we cannot define Zen Buddhists the same way we do in Japan. American students are not priests and yet not completely laymen. I understand it this way: that you are not priests is an easy matter, but that you are not exactly laymen is more difficult. I think you are special people and want some special practice that is not exactly priest's practice and not exactly laymen's practice. You are on your way to discovering some appropriate way of life. I think that is our Zen community, our group.[1]

Suzuki-roshi understood that if Zen practice was to take root in this country, it would have to adapt itself to American culture, and he encouraged his students, including Les, to find that "appropriate way of life." He had many fine students, and even though he died over twenty years ago, they have kept the practice alive and flourishing, each in his or her own way. Most of them have chosen to practice in the various residential Zen centers in the San Francisco Bay Area, and these practice places continue to be sources of strength and support for the entire American Zen community. But someday, when another fifty or seventy-five years have passed and Zen practice has seeped completely into our bones, perhaps the contributions of one Zen student, Les Kaye, will be fully appreciated. His sincere efforts to bring Zen practice into the daily lives of everyday, ordinary people will certainly go down in the annals of Zen as nothing short of revolutionary. This is the best gift he could have given his teacher—and his students.

MISHA MERRILL
Woodside, California

the quest: a parable

Once there was a young girl who tended the forest and valleys of her native home. She loved all living things and continually cared for their well-being. Her greatest joy was working with them, helping them in whatever way she could.

When branches or dead limbs fell into the streams, she cleared them so that the waters could continue to flow and fish could find their way. She removed overgrowth from high trees so that light could reach the forest floor. Where winds and rain eroded the land, she planted new growth to prevent floods. When tall grasses became dry during summer drought, she harvested them to reduce the risk of fire. And when an animal was sick or injured, she treated its wounds and gave it shelter.

One day the girl saw a prince resting in a meadow. He was lying on a comfortable quilt, embroidered with colors of the rainbow. His clothes were of the finest silk. The sun reflected in the radiant jewels adorning his strong, young body. Spread before him was a dazzling array of fruits, nuts, and sweet cakes. Her senses were intoxicated by the ruby color of the wine in the crystal goblet. She thought it was the most beautiful sight she had ever seen.

The prince saw the young girl watching him. He invited her to join him. She was fascinated by the richness of his jewels, excited by the sweet and spicy tastes of his food. She lost herself in the comfort of the prince's soft quilt.

"How did you come by these riches?" she asked.

"You can have them, too," he replied.

"How is that possible? I have never seen such things here in the forest and valleys."

"I will share them with you. But you must first give something to me."

"What is it?" the girl asked with excitement. "I will do anything to have these wonderful things."

"You must get for me the golden crown from the castle at the far end of the world, lying beyond the sea, the mountain, and the jungle. And you must bring me the head of the dragon that roams the ocean, the wings from the eagle that flies over the mountain, and the coat from the lion that rules the jungle. If you bring me these things within one year, we will be married and I will give you all I own."

"But how can I get these things?" she asked. "I know nothing of the ways of the world." The prince gave her a magic spear to kill the dragon, a net to catch the eagle, and a sword to slay the lion.

So, with great excitement, she set out on her adventure to bring back the golden crown and share the riches of the world. She crossed the ocean and killed the dragon with her magic spear, keeping his head to bring to the prince. She climbed the mountain, catching the eagle with her net, keeping his wings. And she entered the jungle, where she killed the lion with her sword, taking his coat for the prince.

As she came closer to the far end of the world, she found herself on a vast, open plain. There were no mountains, no oceans, no jungles, no forests, meadows, or valleys. On the horizon, she could see the castle at the far end of the world. With enthusiasm, she continued her journey. But no matter how quickly she traveled, no matter how many miles she covered each day, she came no closer to the castle. Day after day, the castle remained on the far horizon.

As she traveled, the plain became a desert. Her body became tired, her heart weary and sick. The head of the dragon, the wings of the eagle, and the coat of the lion grew heavier with each step. But still she continued on to the castle at the far end of the world.

At last, the young woman came to an oasis. Exhausted, she fell asleep under the shade of its trees, by the cool water of its clear pond. She was awakened by a humpbacked, one-eyed dwarf sitting a few feet away, watching her.

At first, the young woman was frightened. But because his eye was so clear and his smile so natural, she let go of her fear and opened her heart. She told the dwarf her story and learned that he was the caretaker of the oasis. The dwarf came to her and told her to look into the clear pond. "What do you see?" he asked.

To her surprise, in the waters of the pond, she saw the prince with his beauty, riches, and comforts. She saw all the things she wanted, the reasons for her long and difficult journey. Then the water was rippled by a sudden breeze and the vision faded.

The dwarf said to her, "Now put your hands in the water." As she did, the water cleared again. Now she saw the dragon, the eagle, and the lion. Seeing the creatures she had slain on her quest for the crown, the woman felt remorse and shame. A breeze rippled the water again. When it cleared, she saw her home. But the streams were stagnant; there were no fish, birds, or animals. The forest was dark and silent.

The young woman cried for her home that had died, her tears red as blood. As they fell into the pond, the vision changed once again.

Now she saw the forest streams flowing, the plants, trees, fish, birds, and animals in abundance. And she saw herself wearing the golden crown. The young woman threw the spear, the net, and the sword into the pond. When she did, the dragon, the eagle, and the lion came to life and returned to the ocean, mountain, and jungle.

When she looked up from the pond, the dwarf and the oasis were gone. She was back in the forest, surrounded by beauty and the creatures she loved. She felt the richness and comfort of her own life.

* * *

This parable of journey and homecoming portrays how easily we stray from living in harmony in our natural world. It is about the sickness and suffering that result from mindlessly pursuing desires. In the story, the girl leaves the limitless freedom and unity—the community—of her natural home. Seduced by the promise of sensual pleasures, she separates herself from all she has known, turning away from caring for the creatures of the forest. As she takes up the tools of technology, the immediacy of her loving-kindness is replaced by visions of conquest and pleasure.

Like the girl in the story, we have forgotten the purpose of our lives' activity. We have come to believe that our daily work is something we must do to please others so that we can have wealth, comfort, prestige, and beauty. We think that work must take us far away from ourselves, that it requires us to conquer whatever stands in our way. So we compete and contend with what we meet and take souvenirs to show our accomplishments. We are easily fooled by the excitement of what we think we will attain from our daily battles.

But our faraway goal is never reached. We discover instead that it was an illusion and that we have wandered alone into a desert. We are overcome with spiritual sickness and longing for our home. In desperation, we wake up to face the truth of what we have been doing with our lives. Even though this truth appears ugly and frightening, because we put our trust in it and open our hearts to it, we ultimately recognize the delusion of our quest for riches. By facing the frightening side of ourselves, we are shown our inherently pure nature.

When we misunderstand, when we forget what we should be doing with our lives, we are led astray by the desire for riches and comfort. Thinking we must overcome monsters that stand in our way, we use the magic of modern conveniences and technologies to kill life instead of nurturing it. We carry around the bodies of what we have destroyed until finally we become lost and sick. In this story, the young woman saw, through her tears, what was in her blood. Her real work was taking care of life, not pursuing a golden crown to enhance someone else's royalty. Her mistake—our mistake—is to be mesmerized by someone else's "royalty" and to deny our own.

At work in the modern world, spiritual life includes our own marvelous, mundane activities. It includes treating everyone we meet—our bosses, our co-workers—and everything we do—routine chores as well as major projects—as honored guests. By carefully considering the results of each of our actions, by performing each activity with reverence, as an offering of a gift, we leave no traces, no battle scars.

Spiritual practice is our oasis. It enables us to come home, to renew ourselves, and to let our hearts be open. Practice lets us understand that we are already wealthy, that we already wear the crown. When we give up striving for more riches and great excitement, and give our lives to taking care of life, then life renews itself.

zen

AT WORK

CHAPTER 1

dual careers

These days when I am asked, "Where did you get your Zen training?" I like to say, "IBM." I enjoy the looks of surprise from people who expect me to describe long months of silent meditation in Japanese temples or in retreats on mist-covered mountains. My answer only seems to be in fun. It is, in fact, very serious. A corporate work environment, with its stress, aggressiveness, and bureaucracy, may not seem a likely place to discover the meaning of spiritual activity. Yet when I started Zen practice, IBM was where I worked, where I spent a major part of my life, and where I devoted the biggest portion of my creative energy. Instinctively I knew that I had to make the effort to learn how to "carry water and chop wood" in the complex activities of the modern world. So the high-tech, corporate workplace became my "monastery," where I explored what has become an important, growing question of late-twentieth-century America: how do I express spiritual practice in everyday life?

I went to work for IBM in San Jose in 1956, a few weeks after graduating as an engineer from Cornell. The company had recently opened a major facility at the southern edge of the city. On the huge production floor, engineers and technicians were busily assembling and testing RAMAC, the revolutionary magnetic disk data storage product. RAMAC, the acronym for Random Access Method for Accounting and Control, was the name of one of the earliest high-technology "breakthrough" inventions to come out of California's Santa Clara Valley. RAMAC made it possible for computers to quickly store and retrieve large amounts of information, creating an entirely new industry known as DASD, or direct access storage devices. RAMAC was the forerunner of the hard disk and floppy disk of today's personal computers.

The feeling of this new IBM location was like a small start-up company rather than a vast, forty-year-old corporation. High expectations for the innovative product were almost palpable. I could taste the ozone of excitement in the air. Career prospects seemed unlimited.

In the midfifties, engineering graduates had their pick of jobs. Companies were offering lucrative starting salaries and attractive incentives. I didn't choose IBM for financial reasons; the aircraft industry in Los Angeles, for example, was offering a great deal more money. And smaller companies were offering more freedom. But IBM had certain qualities that I admired, including its reputation for outstanding management, technical leadership, and service to customers. It was also well-known for the strong loyalty and dedication of its employees. I thought it was the perfect location to begin a career: San Jose was only an hour's drive from San Francisco.

California offered "the good life." Gasoline was still twenty-eight cents a gallon. For $25,000, you could buy a spacious ranch-style home in a quiet, clean neighborhood that came equipped with the most ideal climate imaginable. The scenic, agricultural Santa Clara Valley—known as the prune capital of the world— was a new environment for conservative IBM, which up until then had been associated with small-town, upstate New York manufacturing plants; white-shirted, blue-suited salesmen; and the increasingly pervasive punch card. But change was in the air. The first interstate highway was under way, and space exploration was about to begin. It was the start of the Information Age; the "Valley of Heart's Delight" was soon to become "Silicon Valley."

Anticipating this good life, a classmate and I drove from upstate New York to California, with brief stops in New York City and Las Vegas. We rented an apartment not far from downtown San Jose. Like a great many other young men at the time, I had attended ROTC in college. Military orders were handed out on graduation day. That's when I learned that I was to start my two years of active duty just one month after I was scheduled to begin at IBM! On my first day of work, I explained my situation. It was no problem, since it was already understood that I would be taking a military leave of absence. That sort of arrangement between industry and young graduates was fairly common during the "cold war," especially just a few years after the Korean conflict.

Our first assignment at IBM, along with twenty or so other engineers and technicians of varying degrees of experience, was to test the new RAMACs as they completed production. It was challenging work, requiring intense technical training. We spent the first three weeks of our professional careers in a classroom off the main plant site at 99 Notre Dame Avenue, a nondescript industrial building leased by IBM in downtown San Jose. It was here that experienced IBM engineers from Endicott, New York, along with recent graduates from local colleges, had created high-tech history by developing the RAMAC in the early fifties. Until eight o'clock each night, we studied the life force of the RAMAC, which was powered by hundreds of diodes and triodes. Not only did we have to learn how to operate the system and fix its "bugs" but we also had to learn the revolutionary new technology of magnetic disk recording.

When the class ended, we went back to the manufacturing site to test these sophisticated machines, pulsating with the electro-mechanical yet seemingly intelligent life of creatures from science fiction. I was put on a team of experienced troubleshooters. Work was intense amid the constant high-speed whir of the massive disk drive, the reciprocating swoosh-swoosh-swoosh of the mechanical arm moving the magnetic head to its position over the spinning magnetic-coated disks, the blower fans courageously trying to suck out the heat created by the tightly housed, glowing vacuum tubes and their associated electrical circuitry.

I couldn't keep up with the more knowledgeable technicians. Their hands and eyes knew intuitively where to find the bad component or cold solder joint that was causing a problem. I remember one engineer who always seemed to know precisely which tube to tap with his pencil to "fix" a bug! Rarely did any of them need to look at the circuit diagrams that I had studied at 99 Notre Dame. But that's where I had to begin when I went looking for a bug. I was too slow to be of much use; the best I could do was to help whenever I was asked to do something specific, learn what I could by observing, and stay out of the way. The team had a schedule to meet and a rhythm of its own; there wasn't inclination or time to coach the new guy, who was leaving in a week anyway.

For the first time, I was on my own in a confusing, uncertain situation in the "real world." I had just graduated from a respected engineering school, yet I was incompetent on my first job. The experience of summer jobs did not help. I was discouraged, feeling so useless, not able to contribute. I was relieved when the time came for me to leave for the army.

Returning to work two years later, I landed an assignment as a design engineer in the IBM product development laboratory. It was totally different from the short time I'd spent testing RAMACs. I was on a design team with two veteran engineers. Laconic, easygoing Vern liked to wear his glasses at the tip of his nose. He rarely took off his suit jacket, even when he was designing circuits at his desk or testing them in the clutter of the lab. He was a genius at making transistors behave. Art was the mechanical engineer team leader, a dedicated, likable, serious but playful New Yorker. Unlike Vern, Art always had his tie loose and his sleeves rolled up. He was the most pragmatic individual I ever met, insisting on rational explanations for anything having to do with the project. From Art, I learned the importance of examining assumptions, of distinguishing them from what I really knew to be true, and of verifying each assumption, with either experiment or experience. "Gut feelings are a good place to start," he told me, "but don't take anything for granted. Dig out the truth." He was a good mentor, and I was a willing apprentice.

The job of our little team was to develop a technology for handling a radically new IBM punch card. By decreasing the size of the traditional punched hole a full 80 percent, this innovative design tripled the data-carrying capacity of a card. My responsibility was to create a light-sensing method for detecting these very small card holes, which could not be "read" reliably by the old electromechanical method.

This project was the greatest fun I ever had. Not only did we enjoy our time together but we were a huge technical success. Throughout its three years, our work gained the attention of local as well as corporate management. The marketing people were pleased. We were making a great contribution to technology and to the eventual improvement in business productivity. So I was shocked the morning our manager announced that the project was being canceled.

I couldn't believe it. Our team had done everything right; we were poised for success. But we didn't achieve our anticipated "success" because something changed. For weeks I didn't understand what had happened, except that it was a "marketing decision." With dismay, I finally understood that we had been working on an old technology! What had changed was IBM's product strategy. The increasing realization that computers were the way of the future made investing in the creation of a new line of punch card equipment, no matter how innovative, no longer feasible.

It was my first lesson in the most fundamental axiom of the universe: beyond my control, somewhere, somehow, by someone, change is always taking place. My disappointment was immense. "What a waste of time. How could they let this happen?" I asked myself over and over. The disappointment was provided mainly by my own ego. I was upset about the lost success that had seemed so close and so deserved. Yet the disappointing pill was not so terribly bitter after all. No one's job, career, or life was threatened. The project had been a great adventure, I had picked up good experience and established a reputation as a competent engineer.

I had gained much and had lost nothing. In reality, there was no need for disappointment.

By now I had become increasingly drawn to the human dimensions of work and the workplace. I noticed that I was more enthusiastic when working with people rather than with the technology. I was fascinated by the creative impact of communications and information exchange. I decided to pursue my growing interest in business as a whole, as an organic community of individuals, and began studying for an MBA at the new evening program at Santa Clara University.

My managers supported my new direction and offered me an opportunity to join a market research group. In order to have me gain experience in the "real world" of marketing, I was given a two-year special assignment in the IBM sales office in downtown San Jose. After eighteen months, I was surprised and pleased to be offered a job as manager of a systems analysis department in the product development laboratory on the plant site. I finished my MBA, and at age thirty I was very satisfied with the way my career was going. But in ways that I was not aware of, my attitude toward work and life was changing. The foundation of this change had been established many years earlier.

When I was very young, my spiritual awareness was limited to a foggy sense of the presence of "something bigger" than me and my personal life. During grammar school years, I was intent on trying to discover this elusive something. I was convinced that "it" was the primary source of life and of everything in the world. I hoped to end my spiritual confusion by understanding this "source" and clarify the meaning of my life. My method for trying to understand this fundamental essence was to examine intellectually all the reasons I could think of for the universe to exist and to try to envision what had "existed" before the universe came into being.

Analytical thinking only created more confusion. On the one hand, if there was nothing before creation, I thought, how could the "something" of the universe come from "nothing"? On the other hand, if there was something before the creation of the world, it must have always existed, without beginning. But how could "something" have no starting point, no first moment? I was frustrated by these questions, and by not being able to envision the timelessness that went with "no beginning." As a boy, I was continually preoccupied by such attempts to explain the world rationally. I was unable to recognize or accept the limitation of my logical mind, its inability to understand the nature of life beyond concepts of solid objects and linear time.

I did not pursue these dim spiritual inclinations. Instead, I dismissed them as childhood fantasies. I thought they were "weird" feelings that I had better keep to myself. Yet, as an adult many years later, I wept spontaneously when I saw reproductions of the 20,000-year-old cave paintings at Lascaux in Central France. I was at a loss to explain the tears—I felt no sadness, nor any other emotion. The graphic memory of that moment remained with me for months as I became aware of the origin of the feeling aroused by those paintings of wild, prehistoric bulls and horses. It was the joy of recognition, as in the discovery of a long-lost family. The vividness of this experience, of this connection, confirmed that I was part of something that transcended ideas of space and time.

During my last year of college, I had the opportunity to take a few classes unrelated to engineering. Having been so heavily involved in the physical sciences for so long, I discovered an appetite for the nonanalytic, intuitive, and passionate literary world. I was surprised by my enthusiasm. In particular, I was fascinated by Greek tragedies, especially the myth of Prometheus. In this legend, Prometheus takes pity on the crude human race and gives it the gift of fire. His courageous act enrages Zeus, who binds him to a rock, where an eagle tears open his flesh each day. I was absorbed by this image of the hero who sacrifices his own freedom and well-being to save mankind.

Later that year, I read *The Catcher in the Rye* and was struck by the taking-care attitude of the would-be hero. Holden Caulfield envisions himself as a savior of children:

> Anyway, I keep picturing all these kids playing some game in this big field of rye and all. Thousands of little kids, and nobody's around—nobody big, I mean—except me. And I'm standing on the edge of some crazy cliff. What I have to do, I have to catch everybody if they start to go over the cliff—I mean if they're running and don't look where they're going I have to come out from somewhere and catch them. That's all I'd do all day. I'd just be the catcher in the rye and all. I know it's crazy, but that's the only thing I'd really like to be.[1]

The compassion of the determined, selfless hero of the ancient Greek myth seemed no different to me from that of the confused young man of the 1950s. Prometheus acts out of his feelings and willingly suffers as a result. Holden is unable to act and only vaguely feels something that he dismisses as "crazy." Yet Holden's sense of compassion is real, even though it has not found a way of expression. He wants to save children who "don't look where they're going," who are too busy playing to pay attention, to recognize the dangers of an unaware life. It is a perfect Buddhist metaphor for the delusions of humanity. I did not recognize the Bodhisattva[2] image in Holden's vision of the catcher. But later I learned that J. D. Salinger had explored Mahayana Buddhism and reflected it in much of his writing.

During Thanksgiving weekend in 1958, a few months after I had returned to San Jose and civilian life, I flew to Los Angeles to visit my college classmate, who had left IBM. I was almost the last person to board the plane. When I did, I immediately took the seat next to Mary, a slender, dark-haired young woman. I couldn't believe that the seat was still empty. She was more than pretty.

Her eyes were bright with quiet self-awareness. Her mouth expressed kindness and readiness to smile. Her presence reflected confidence and poise. She said that she worked at Mills Hospital in San Mateo. I repeated it over and over in my mind: "Mills Hospital, San Mateo. Mills Hospital, San Mateo."

Mary was also on her way to visit a friend. The plane was two hours late leaving San Francisco, landing us at Los Angeles International after 2:00 A.M. By that time, the bus that had brought her friend to the airport had stopped running. My friend and I offered them a ride to her friend's home. Although not by design, our route home was indirect. Distracted by the excitement of old friends reuniting, we got lost somewhere between the airport and Pasadena. At 5:00 A.M., we finally stopped for breakfast at a delicatessen on Sunset Boulevard. The next week, Mary and I had our first date. We were married in August of the following year.

In the fall of 1961, at a Friday evening cocktail party, I found Alan Watts's The Way of Zen on my hostess's bookshelf.[3] I had heard about Zen but never read about it. The book caught my attention; I borrowed it over the weekend. At the time, Mary and I were living in a two-room cottage on a 900-acre pear ranch just off Skyline Boulevard, near Los Gatos. The autumn days were chilly and damp. On Saturday morning, I lit a fire, and for most of the next two days I immersed myself in Watts's spellbinding description of the history and practice of Zen. I was fascinated to discover a dimension of living, an attitude about life, that I had not known before. When I closed the book, I knew that my technically oriented, mainstream life was incomplete, that it alone could not provide the balance I was seeking. Watts's description struck a chord of authenticity. It told me that Zen Buddhism held the missing elements and, in ways that I didn't yet understand, pointed to the "source" that I had sought years earlier.

It was the time between the "Beat Generation" and the "hippie" era. Alan Watts was a regular feature on a local PBS radio station. I became a devoted listener and read almost everything he wrote. The extent of my interest in Zen was limited to reading and talking about it. I assumed that in order to be fully involved in Zen, it would be necessary to live in Japan for several years. For me, that was not a realistic option. I planned to raise a family and continue my career just where I was.

In the fall of 1966, I was startled by an article in the *Chronicle* that described the San Francisco Zen Center, amazed to discover that actual Zen practice had been taking place for several years close to home. A few weeks later, following a business meeting in the city, I located the Zen Center in the neighborhood known as Japantown.

Expecting a quiet, secluded, Japanese-style temple, I encountered instead a turn-of-the-century concrete building facing the noisy traffic of Bush Street. The unlocked front door was guarded by two tablets. To the left, in stone, were chiseled the Ten Commandments in Hebrew: the building was originally a synagogue. On a wooden block to the right of the door was some Japanese calligraphy: the building was now the home of the Japanese-American Zen Buddhist congregation.

I entered the old, musty structure. The dim hallway was quiet. The smell of incense mingled with another familiar, ancient fragrance: chicken soup. Or so I thought. Later I was to find out that it was the aroma of Japanese miso soup. I opened a door and entered a small office, encountering an elderly Japanese man, wearing a hat, reading a Japanese-language newspaper. He paid no attention to me. I thought, "Is that the Zen master?" On the other side of the office were two very tall, very bald young men, operating a hand-crank mimeograph machine.

I asked about Zen practice. One of them said: "Just sit." I had no idea what he meant. I glanced at the man reading the newspaper. "Is that the Zen master?" I wondered again. I explained to the two young men that I lived in San Jose, fifty miles south of San Francisco. They told me about an affiliated meditation group closer to home in Los Altos, where the abbot of the San Francisco center, Zen Master Suzuki-roshi, traveled each Wednesday evening to lecture and lead meditation.[4]

In early December 1966, Mary and I found ourselves at Haiku Zendo, a meditation hall created from the garage of the home of Marian Derby. Its name was derived from its seventeen permanent spaces for meditation, the number of syllables in a Japanese haiku poem. The room could be made to accommodate up to thirty people, using additional meditation cushions on the floor. Marian gave us basic instructions in zazen, seated Zen meditation.

That first evening was difficult. The unheated meditation hall, or zendo, was freezing. Our legs and backs were cramped and sore. Understanding Suzuki-roshi, whose English was still tentative, was difficult. He spoke a great deal about "pedrachs." Years later, we figured out that he meant "patriarchs." On the drive home, we agreed, "Never again, that's too painful." Nonetheless, we returned the following Wednesday.

What brought us back? Partly it was Suzuki-roshi's quiet confidence and gentle humor. His words conveyed something fundamentally true that I didn't quite understand, and his manner expressed and encouraged trust. In addition, Marian made us feel very welcome. Despite the discomfort, I sensed something subtle in the activity of zazen, which ironically did not seem to involve any activity at all, except trying to sit still and be quiet.

We commuted from San Jose to Haiku Zendo two or three times a week. The Wednesday evening schedule included meditation and lecture, with tea and a chance for socializing afterward. Suzuki-roshi and Katagiri-roshi alternated coming from San Francisco Zen Center on Wednesdays and staying overnight in Marian's home.[5] Thursday morning included meditation, a short lecture, and an informal breakfast in the dining room.

A Saturday morning schedule provided an opportunity to experience the basic forms of traditional Zen monastic practice. It included two periods of zazen, beginning at 5:30 A.M., breakfast in the meditation hall, a work period, and a meditation at 9:00 A.M.

Greeting the first light of dawn in silent zazen continues to be a quietly profound experience. I fell in love with the formal monastic-style breakfast, using traditional Zen monks' eating bowls known as *oryooki*.[6] I was so inspired by this reverential, ceremonial way of serving, receiving, and eating meals that I eventually wrote a small book about the construction and use of oryooki.

The work was simple: we brushed off the meditation cushions, dusted the corners, mopped the floor, cleaned the altar, swept outside, and washed dishes. Sometimes we helped Marian with yardwork. The Saturday work period was an important element of the practice at Haiku Zendo. Not only did it allow us to repay Marian for her generosity but it also enabled us to take care of our communal practice place. The latter reflects a crucial point of spiritual practice: its giving nature, its orientation toward others. Other key elements of Zen practice—zazen, study, and being with the teacher—are at risk of becoming self-oriented activities if not balanced by the practice of giving time and effort to others, to taking care of the community, giving up any notion of personal benefit from doing the work.

Soon after we started going to Haiku Zendo, Mary and I bought our own cushions and began our weekdays with zazen in our San Jose living room. In June of 1967, we participated in our first one-day meditation retreat at the San Francisco Zen Center. During the break following lunch, we took a walk on Bush Street. The early summer day was cool and clear; a gentle breeze came from the bay. Mary said, "It's too nice to go back to that dark room." So we drove to Sausalito and spent the afternoon drinking beer and eating hamburgers on the deck of Zack's, a pub that shared the lagoon with houseboats and seagulls.

true nature

I had a very short career as an IBM salesman. After I had been in the sales office for just over a year, I was asked to "prospect," to visit businesses in one of San Jose's older neighborhoods to identify and gain the interest of potential IBM customers. During the previous several months, I had completed IBM's sales and systems engineering training program, one of the most successful in the world. But despite my new marketing skills and the backing of IBM's reputation, I had a hard time lining up prospects.

I was troubled by the idea of actively trying to sell a product or a service to another person. I did not trust aggressive selling, feeling that it is intrusive, that it manipulates people through clever words, taking advantage of their weaknesses and their insecurities. I felt that people should be left alone to recognize for themselves what they need without having to be told or sold.

Yet I knew that there is nothing inherently wrong with selling. I recognized that it is a vital element of any cohesive community. In the marketplaces of earlier societies, in the modern department store, or in private, face-to-face negotiations, selling continues to be a fundamental way for people to exchange and share, to support each other with what they have to offer. I knew that selling can be creative and beneficial, if approached with integrity and thoughtfulness.

As a result of my conflicting feelings, I had trouble getting started as a salesman. I was aware that I had something to resolve.

During my first week of "prospecting," I got nowhere with the small companies in the pre–World War II industrial section of town. I couldn't get past the reception desks. I didn't know if my lack of success was caused by my resistance and fear of selling, poor technique, or simply being at the wrong place at the wrong time. For several days, I was discouraged, until finally, one morning, the office manager of a family-owned paving and gravel company accepted my offer to survey his business procedures to determine if automation would save time and money.

During the next week, the clerks and foremen showed me how their company manually handled its finances, its inventory, and the status of its jobs. I developed a new set of procedures for managing their information, based on the use of IBM's punch card equipment. Problem solving was the easy and enjoyable part— creating procedural flow diagrams and the analysis that showed time and dollar savings. But in the back of my mind was a nagging anxiety about making a "sales pitch."

First of all, there was fear, which I supposed was natural for a beginning salesman. I was afraid they wouldn't accept my proposal; I didn't like the prospect of being turned down, of hearing the dreaded *no*. But my anxiety didn't make logical sense. People at the paving company were pleased that I was studying their procedures and looked forward to my presentation. I knew that my fears were irrational and that it would be a mistake to give in to them, to run away, for example, by pleading to my sales manager, "I'm not a salesman, I'm an engineer! Get a more experienced guy to make the pitch!"

So I simply continued what I was doing, deciding that the best way to overcome my fear was to go into as much detail as was needed to convince myself that the system I was developing would really benefit the company. I learned something very interesting about fear: it arose only when I thought about the possible negative impact on me—will I fail? will I make a fool of myself?— rather than about the work and the potential positive effect on the company. As long as I kept my mind on what I was doing, I was OK.

I noticed something else about my reluctance. I was developing my analysis and sales approach from a single viewpoint: my own. On paper, I was sure that I could demonstrate how the use of IBM equipment would result in cost savings. But this would be the company's first venture into automation. I didn't know how they felt, emotionally, about such a major change. So I started to spend more time with the office manager and his staff, trying to understand their feelings about the business and its future. As I modified my sales approach to include their expectations and concerns, my anxiety diminished almost completely. I looked forward to making my sales pitch.

It almost worked. My sales presentation confidently demonstrated increased efficiency, better service, and money in the bank for this company. Everyone was pleased, with one exception. Until the day of my presentation, I had not met the key decision maker, the owner of the company, a man in his eighties who rarely came into the office because of a disability. Despite the logic of my analysis, his "gut feel" told him something else: the time was not right for a change. In my inexperience and eagerness to make the presentation, I had not recognized the necessity, the wisdom, of understanding the minds and gaining the confidence of everyone, without exception.

So I didn't close the sale. I felt disappointed not to succeed after all my struggles, another encounter with discouragement and the workings of my mind. However, the seeds were planted. Within a few years, the company began an extensive program of automation with IBM.

world without boundaries

Our inherent nature, what is known in Buddhism as our true nature, is without limit, so vast that it includes everything. It means that we, ourselves, include everything and at the same time that we are included in everything. But it is impossible to appreciate our lives in this way by just thinking about them with our rational minds. If we use only our analytic capacity to try to understand our lives and the world we live in, we will overlook the vastness of our true world, the world of our true nature. The limitless world, the world without boundaries, cannot be reached by thinking.

The thinking mind constantly comes up against the limits of what it knows at some particular moment. As we make our efforts in daily life to understand situations and solve various problems, we increase our knowledge and push back the boundaries of what we know about our everyday world. And as our knowledge and experience grow wider, the limits expand. Yet even as the thinking mind expands the limit of what it knows, it comes up against boundaries. And because that is its everyday experience, it believes that the entire world inherently has boundaries. But a world of boundaries is a made-up world, created by the limitations of our rational minds.

When we envision a world of boundaries, we logically presume that it must have a center. The small mind—the ego—then tries to make itself the center of this world. But it is impossible to stand in the center of a made-up world. When we try to stand in this imaginary center, we feel off balance and anxious. We attempt to relieve our anxiety by filling our made-up world with material and emotional things. We may even try to obtain enlightenment. However, enlightenment does not exist in a world of boundaries, a made-up world. Enlightenment exists in the world without limits, the vast world that shows itself when we are not trying to be at the center. The point of Zen practice is to let go of ideas about boundaries and to feel our limitless true nature. When we express our limitless true minds, we understand that there are no boundaries and no center. Then we are no longer concerned about being the center.

When we first feel limitless mind, we may also feel various emotions, such as anger, sadness, or discouragement. These feelings are just the small mind trying to be the center. Our egos do not want to give up their world of boundaries because they do not want to give up ideas about themselves. So if we feel discouraged, it is just the stubbornness of our thinking minds. Even if we feel stubbornness, the best thing to do is to continue mindfulness and stay aware of what we are feeling. There is no need to turn away from limitlessness because we feel some emotion. We only need to continue with confidence and let ourselves drop into the world of no limits.

In the limitless world, we do not know where we are going. But this is not a problem because inherently we have nowhere to go. When we feel our limitlessness, we just move in the direction of Big Mind, the mind that includes everything. In the limitless world, we just let Big Mind be our guide.

Big Mind can appear when our hearts start to open and our concerns turn from ourselves to others. Then our true nature can express itself. When we feel our minds turn from "inside" to "outside," we should move in that direction, toward compassion and the relief of suffering. To do so, we have to make an effort not to become side-tracked by ideas of comfort or pleasure or desire. Otherwise, we will create a limited, made-up world again.

Desires are very strong. Like drugs, they promise us excitement and comfort, but they fool us, so that we want to make our efforts only for ourselves. A life driven by desire creates serious problems for us and for others. So when desire appears, we continue observing the thinking mind trying to fool itself. We watch how it tries to create boundaries and establish itself as the center. When we become aware of what our mind is doing, we should make an effort to let go of the boundaries and of ourself as the center of some small world. Our spiritual practice is to let the mind be wide so that it can resume its vastness. Then we can express our true selves and give ourselves to life and to others.

nothing to catch

In Zen practice, we do not try to obtain anything, not even peace of mind. Trying to obtain something for our minds actually disturbs our peace of mind. Ironically, by trying to obtain peace of mind, we lose it. Only when we do not try to obtain it can we have peace of mind.

It is impossible to obtain what we already possess. Similarly, we cannot express what we already possess if we are trying to obtain it. So if we feel discouraged in our practice, it is an indication that we are trying to obtain something for our minds rather than expressing what we already have. Zen practice expresses what we inherently possess.

Inherently, every one of us has complete wisdom. But because we do not understand our fundamental nature, we strive to obtain wisdom and concern ourselves with having some experience of it. The point of our practice is simply to give inherent wisdom a chance. We begin by trusting it. And in order to trust inherent wisdom, we first have to trust ourselves. Practice must begin with deep trust in ourselves. If we emphasize obtaining something for our minds, it means that we do not trust ourselves or our inherent wisdom. So we practice zazen to let go of self-oriented ideas. This is the basis for trusting ourselves and for giving inherent wisdom a chance.

Inherent wisdom is real; it is Reality itself. However, it cannot come from emphasizing something substantial, something material that we can recognize with our rational, everyday minds. Everyday mind is limited to things of the phenomenal world, things of form and color and sound and feelings. By contrast, the basis of wisdom is our true nature, which everyday mind cannot reach. If we try to obtain wisdom or happiness, we are attempting to grasp something that cannot be held like a physical object. This kind of effort leads only to disappointment.

Imagine a child trying to catch a soap bubble. After playing with bubbles for a short time, the child learns their nature. He understands that they are insubstantial and gives up trying to catch them. He understands the nature of bubbles without thinking about it. He doesn't say to himself, "I understand. These bubbles have no permanent nature." Just watching and playing with them, the child understands and enjoys them as they are. But if the child cannot understand the nature of bubbles through his experience, he will continue to try to catch them and will become unhappy when he cannot.

It is fruitless for us to try to grasp wisdom or peace of mind. We should simply let practice be the basis of our lives. Then our inherent wisdom can reveal itself. Then we can realize our inherent completeness and we can see that there is no need to obtain or grasp anything. That is how we learn to appreciate and enjoy bubbles.

Giving up grasping does not mean giving up the activities of our daily lives. And it does not mean that we live aimlessly by not taking care of things and the responsibilities that we have to each other and the world. It simply means that we let our lives be living continuations of activities. An activity is alive for us when we give ourselves up in its midst, just letting ourselves be the activity without trying to obtain something for our minds. When we do that, we feel the joy of doing something free from desire. Then we feel enlivened and refreshed. That is real freedom.

Our lives do not belong to us. We are just taking care of them. So our practice is to give up our self-oriented view of life, to give up trying to obtain things for our minds, and to understand how to truly take care of whatever comes along. Then we can enjoy the bubbles.

CHAPTER 3

mind and body

inherent unity

When we place our bodies and our minds in the traditional zazen posture, we are expressing the inherent unity of all things. Oneness is our fundamental nature, but it is impossible to fully appreciate and experience ourselves in this way by using only the thinking quality of our minds. Trying to understand our lives through our intellects alone, we look right past our unity and fail to recognize our true selves. Instead, from what our senses tell us, we logically conclude that, fundamentally, we are all separate beings. Out of this misunderstanding our minds create a sense of isolation, resulting in anxiety.

Our unified body-minds are the vehicles of our understanding. They are simultaneously the way we understand how to express our understanding. Usually, "understanding" is viewed as a mental activity, based on an exchange of ideas and words. So when we read or hear something that we intellectually or emotionally accept, we say, "I understand," and when we speak or write something that others accept, we say, "They understand." However, we should be aware that this perception of understanding, a creation of our thinking minds, is based on a subtle notion of separation of "me" from "you," "I" from "they." This is a limited view.

Complete understanding is expressed in our activity, not just in our words or ideas. This is the foundation of Zen practice. Complete understanding includes our entire beings, resting on the oneness of body-mind. The activity of practice expresses this unity. When our attitude is sincere, our posture must also reflect sincerity, or confidence, or our practice will be incomplete. And when we have a determined physical posture, we also need to have a sincere attitude.

In other words, in spiritual practice, the posture and activity of our bodies reflect the attitude of our minds.

Practice is the effort we make to express the unity of body-mind. We try not to let the mind wander, and we try not to let the body wander. Together they express our confidence and determination. Taking care of our bodies means taking care of our minds. In the same way, when we take care of our minds, we take care of our bodies. When we take care of body-mind, we take care of the world. Zazen is the practice of dropping off subtle notions of separation of body from mind and of self from others.

It is not easy to let go of notions of separateness. Throughout the world, individuals as well as entire cultures continue to believe that remaining separate from each other is necessary for safety and wellbeing. So people, races, and nations remain apart and contend against each other. Peace can begin only when we put an end to our own personal separations of body-mind. When we do this, we understand the unity of everything, that we are not separate from the truth.

At work and in other circumstances of daily life, we cannot do all the things that we want to do. We have to determine those activities that we can do, those that we have to postpone, and those that we cannot do in the near future, or perhaps at all. To make these choices we have to consider each potential activity individually—its value and cost to ourselves—as well as its relationship to all others. In addition to establishing these priorities, we have to determine how we will take care of the activities we choose to do, providing the highest quality of work that we can while completing the tasks in a timely manner. These factors determine how well we can create gifts with our effort.

When we choose to perform an activity, we make it a gift by dedicating our entire body-minds to it, by making it the only task we do at that moment. In that way, all activities are included in one and all activities are unified. This is how our activity fills the universe and how we express complete understanding in our work.

Activities of daily life are not separate or isolated. Each is the expression of the entire world. Completing an activity at work only because someone else demands that we do so is not enough to provide us long-term satisfaction. We can be fully satisfied in our work only when we understand that it is the continuation of something that does not end.

If we remove the feathers of a bird's wing in order to study them, we may gain a great deal of knowledge about feathers. But the bird will not be able to fly. Each feather is unique, yet in order to be a wing, all must give themselves as gifts by giving up separateness. They must express inherent unity. Then the bird can fly and can express itself.

the source of carelessness: a story

My first experience at programming a computer came in 1962, while I was working in the IBM sales office, helping salesmen take care of customer accounts. One customer, a large wholesaler of office supplies, discovered a minor bug in one of the programs that created monthly accounting reports. I was asked to fix it.

A few months earlier, during my training as a systems engineer, I had scored very high on IBM's programmer aptitude test. But despite my inherent programming skill, I was impatient when it came to doing the work that evening. It was late, I wanted to get the job over with, I was anxious to get home. I hurried through the programming and implemented a fix without fully testing it. The next day, I received an irritated call from the customer's accounting manager: the "fix" didn't work. I had to go back to his office and do it over. It wasn't a major business problem and didn't create a crisis, but it was careless work that inconvenienced the customer, embarrassing myself as well as IBM.

Coming face to face with anxiety, I had looked the other way, seeking comfort. I had hoped to get away with it, but I didn't, because I was held accountable. Unfortunately, it was by someone else, not me. If I had held myself accountable and fully completed the work on that small task, I would not have created a bigger problem and left a mess, for myself as well as others. This episode demonstrated the role of self-accountability as an expression of spiritual practice in daily affairs. When no one else is holding us accountable—when we have no fear of sanction or embarrass-ment, when we know that we can get away with not doing some-thing that we know that we should do—we maintain our integrity and create a gift for others by holding ourselves accountable for our work. This is the basis of selflessness. This incident taught me the foolishness and the danger of running away from anxiety.

breathing

Zen Master Dogen provides explicit instructions about zazen pos-ture and breathing in his treatise *Fukanzazengi*, Rule for Zazen.[1] But he is not specific about what we should do with our minds. He simply says to "think of not-thinking" by "non-thinking," and that "the essential art of zazen" is "non-thinking." What is this "non-thinking"? How do we do it? How do we know when we are doing it? Dogen doesn't say. But in his few lines about "non-thinking," he tells us to take a deep breath.

When we begin zazen, we take a deep breath to settle our minds. In our daily lives as well, we sometimes take a deep breath to calm our-selves if we feel excited or upset. Taking a deep breath helps us not to do or say something in haste. But deep breath is not just for tense sit-uations. Every breath should be a deep breath.

When we breathe deeply, our breath is complete. There are no traces, no leftovers. When we take a deep breath, our bodies breathe deeply; they are relaxed and ready. At the same time, our deep breath enables our minds to be relaxed and ready. So when our bodies breathe deeply, our minds breathe deeply. Dogen said, "Non-thinking is thinking of not-thinking." Logically this statement makes no sense. "Non-thinking" is both not thinking and *not* trying not to think. So this "non-thinking" is quite subtle because it is both "not-thinking" as well as *not* "not-thinking." In other words, non-thinking is simply the fundamental activity of our minds, the activity that exists before thinking occurs. Dogen means we should let our minds be their fundamental selves, before there is a state of "thinking" and before there is a state of "not-thinking."

Non-thinking mind and deep breath go together; we cannot have one without the other. When we have non-thinking mind, our bodies automatically breathe deeply; we don't have to make a special effort. In *Fukanzazengi*, Dogen instructs us to begin zazen by taking a deep breath. In this way, our bodies calm our minds. But we can also try it the other way, letting our minds calm our bodies. In zazen, or in the activities of daily life, we can let our minds resume "non-thinking," their inherent calmness. Then our breath will be very deep and our bodies will be calm.

Dogen explains the way we should hold our bodies in zazen so our breath can flow uninterrupted and unhindered. He describes zazen posture as the fundamental activity of our bodies before there is activity. So his *Fukanzazengi* describes the activity of our minds before thinking and the activity of our bodies before physical activity.

In non-thinking, the mind breathes deeply. When the mind breathes deeply, all things go their own way. When the mind breathes deeply, it is expressing its fundamental activity, so that when it needs to think, it can do so with a background of calmness.

Sometimes it is necessary for us to use our will, our intention, and sometimes we should just leave things alone, just be with them and watch them. There is a time to think and a time to not think; a time to talk and a time to remain silent; a time to intervene and a time to not interfere; a time to breathe in and a time to breathe out. When all things have their own time, then we have non-thinking. So we let the breath teach the mind and we let the mind teach the breath. When our minds are expressing their fundamental activity of non-thinking, we are aware of everything, everything is aware of everything. Everything breathes deeply with everything. This is spiritual practice and our way of life.

the right cushion

When we practice mindfulness continuously, we have a chance to be aware when the causes of conflict begin to arise in our minds. By becoming aware of them, we have a chance to let them go, to let our minds be free from them. But if we are not aware of them, we will carry them around, letting ourselves be sources of potential conflict and confusion.

Letting go of causes of conflict that arise in our minds does not mean that we give up working to confront injustice when we see it. Rather, it means that we do not try to eliminate injustice when our own minds are full of internal conflict. We should work to eliminate conflict or injustice with peaceful minds. If we don't have peaceful minds when we face injustice, we may create more conflict and more injustice.

Wherever we find ourselves is a good place. Wherever we sit zazen is a good seat. There is no such thing as a bad seat and there is no such thing as a bad cushion. Sometimes when we sit down in zazen posture, we may feel discomfort in our bodies. So we try another cushion that feels more natural. This is fine; we should use cushions that help our posture. But if we still have discomfort after finding what we feel is a good cushion, we should just sit with it.

If we concern ourselves too much with the idea that we need a "better" cushion, we create a conflict in our minds. So we just sit with the cushion that we have right now and make our best effort with it. After the zazen period, we can modify our cushion or find another one, but when we are sitting, any idea about needing a "better" cushion will only disturb our minds. When we let go of these ideas as they arise, our minds will turn from discomfort to selflessness, to feeling grateful for the cushion that we have.

Maybe we are feeling energetic; maybe we are sleepy, hungry, angry, or anxious. It mkes no difference; when we practice, we just practice. Thinking, "I could practice better if only I weren't feeling tired" is the same as wishing for a "better" cushion. Independent of how we feel in our bodies or minds, we practice completely as best we can, wherever we find ourselves, with whatever cushion we are on.

Zen practice is not designed to make us feel either comfortable or uncomfortable. We practice just to express our true nature, which doesn't care about comfort or discomfort, or about any other feeling. We practice without being distracted by such ideas.

The point of our practice is to understand who we are and what all things are and to express the true relationship between ourselves and everything that appears in the world. The problem for us as human beings is that we become confused by our everyday relationships. We do not understand the nature of the true relationship between people and between people and things. Because we are confused by everyday relationships, we create conflict and suffering. Even though everyday relationships are always changing, they are based on the true relationship that does not change. Everyday relationships should be established with an empty mind, a mind that is free from confusion, that understands the nature of true relationship.

Our job in this life is to enable people and things to establish relationships according to capacities and circumstances and according to their true nature. Our job is to encourage this true expression naturally, without getting in the way. When we find something getting in the way, we try to remove it. So we should fit ourselves on whatever cushion we find under us. We should fit ourselves with whomever we are with and whatever situation we are in. This is how we continue Buddha's way in the everyday world.

self-expression

trusting our fundamental question

It isn't necessary for us to know precisely how we begin to sense our spiritual nature. Awareness may grow out of intellectual curiosity, concern for suffering, or a feeling about the mystery of life. It may come from serious reflection about social problems. Or it may develop as a result of our anxiety and confusion.

All the possible paths that lead us to explore spirituality share one thing: a perception that there is something greater than the physical and emotional world. It is important that we not dismiss that kind of feeling, because it arises from our fundamental question about the nature of life. All of us, without exception, want to understand the meaning of life. Whether or not we are consciously aware of it, our minds are continually reflecting on that vital, universal question.

Zen practice enables us to examine life in a very large way, to understand its meaning, and to recognize what is unfolding in our personal lives. Practice makes us intimate with our own difficulties and the difficulties that all human beings encounter, as well as with the source of both confusion and joy.

Although we may not think so, our feeling of something greater than ourselves is an indication that we are already "seeing" something greater and "being" something greater than our personal day-to-day lives. This feeling is the foundation for resolving our question about life. Even though the question arises from our rational minds, they cannot answer their own questions. We can only answer our question through continuous spiritual practice.

We can learn to trust our innermost feelings by allowing intellectual activity to rest and by setting aside personal desires. This trust is the basis of Zen practice.

starting with ourselves

I think that people become interested in Zen practice because of some difficulty or question about life. Personal suffering and concern for meaning are natural starting points for spiritual practice. Having the determination to face our difficulty and the willingness to look directly and honestly at confusion is actually the beginning of understanding.

We need, though, to be careful to recognize that spiritual practice is not just a method for resolving personal problems. The important point is simply to practice without trying to attain something for ourselves or free ourselves from some difficulty. This is true even if we feel that solving our personal problem will benefit other people as well as ourselves. If we carry a goal in mind when we practice, our view of life will be very narrow and we will not be able to come face to face with our difficulty or question. Our minds can be very wide only when practice is not based on an idea of personal attainment. So we must be aware of any tendency to want to solve our personal problems through spiritual practice.

Actually, difficulties in our lives can be opportunities. They give us the chance to see how our minds emphasize desires and personal concerns. Before we have this awareness of our delusions, we remain entangled by old beliefs and habits. That is why we emphasize awareness and acceptance of any difficulties that arise.

When we start zazen practice, our personal concerns may feel intensified. If current concerns do seem sharper and if we become aware of new ones as well, we may think that zazen is making things worse! Naturally, this feeling can be confusing and discouraging. But despite how we may feel, we have to make an effort to trust our practice and continue with determination.

Despite what our common sense may tell us, all things are inherently without difficulty. Everything, everyone, is originally enlightened. This is the fundamental teaching of Buddhism and what we discover for ourselves in our practice. We practice zazen to express this truth.

one circle: a story

"Have you guys seen the marketing surveys?" the boss asked with a big grin on her face. I was part of a group of technical writers developing documentation for users of IBM software. We had gathered for a meeting to review the results of the latest customer satisfaction survey of our work.

"No, haven't seen it," someone said.

"What's it look like?" another asked.

"Just great!" She beamed, obviously delighted.

We went over the results of the survey. They were very good. It was always a relief when marketing surveys showed that our users—the IBM customers—were satisfied with the various printed manuals and computer on-line documentation we provided for them. Yet, except for the manager, none of us was terribly excited. Despite the good news, there was a distinct lack of enthusiasm in the room.

It wasn't that we were smug or pleased with ourselves, expecting nothing less than these glowing reports. It was something more fundamental; a key element was missing in our relationship to our work. Even though as a group of writers we enjoyed what we did as well as working with each other, we did not feel inspired.

This incident took place when I had been with IBM over thirty years. I had been in Zen practice for all except the first few years of my working career. Both experiences contributed to my understanding of this situation in a very large sense. I could see it from the business standpoint as well as from a spiritual perspective.

I sensed that our problem was one of separation. There were invisible boundaries between us and our users that could only be removed by establishing personal relationships and trust. It was an awareness that had been refined by years of zazen practice. We were in our "circle," and they were in theirs.

I was certain that the users, though they reported being satisfied with our documentation, were not enthusiastic about it. However, I needed evidence to verify my hunch. So I asked the other writers if they would like to visit customers, to learn firsthand how our documentation was being used and to discuss, in person, ideas for improvement. Everyone was excited about the idea. Next, I spoke with the IBM sales representatives of several customers who used our product. They confirmed that the customers were interested in talking to the technical writers. Eventually, we visited twelve companies, meeting with programmers and other users who relied on our documentation.

The visitation project was highly successful. Users appreciated our personal interest in their needs and the effort we made to listen to them. They were enthusiastic, had specific concerns for us to resolve and suggestions for us to think about, and asked carefully considered questions. Our personal interest enabled them to see IBM as people, not as a giant corporation. In turn, as a result of meeting with them face to face, the IBM writers felt more confident in understanding the users' requirements. For both sides, the dynamic discussions were far more effective than impersonal survey forms and questionnaires. Subsequently, other writing groups organized visits with their own customers.

The *apparent* business objective of these visits was to gain information about the needs of our users. But that was just one of its goals, the rational explanation to justify the time and business expense. My real motive was to create a more collaborative relationship. In other words, I saw that we had not so much an information problem as a "boundary" problem. I wanted us to invite ourselves into our customers' circle, and them into ours.

If we are asked how to express spiritual practice in everyday life, we could, based on this kind of story, give a Zen-like answer: "Make one circle." But spiritual practice has nothing to do with clever sayings. It begins with recognizing that our so-called everyday life is already spiritual and what we must do is treat it with reverence. Expressing spirituality in everyday affairs is based on our attitude toward our activities and relationships rather than on trying to figure out "how" to do it.

Some people say that Zen is not for everyone, but I don't believe that is so. It may seem true if Zen is understood only as a tough-guy, samurai-oriented form of practice. But Zen as an expression of Buddhism, grounded in the relief of suffering, has a gentle, accommodating dimension. It is not intended to be a confrontation or a contest, either with ourselves or with others.

Ancient Buddhists were very wise. They understood that change is difficult for people to accept and that the best way to introduce something new is to let it become part of something familiar, something that people already trust. They knew that the best thing to do was to have patience, to let people proceed at their own pace.

If there is a physical difficulty in practice, there is no fundamental need to sit cross-legged on a cushion; a chair is fine. Even in the meditation hall, lying down for zazen is acceptable in the case of a severe back problem; other people will accommodate. In the middle of a meditation period, if someone truly feels she must stand up and leave, it's OK. We don't need to shout, "Sit down!" or "Where are you going?" We just trust that people know what is best for them.

Someone may be having emotional difficulty, his busy mind wrestling with a bitter memory. In such a case, extended periods of motionless quiet may cause old, painful feelings to reappear, creating great upset. There is no need to insist that thirty or forty

minutes of silent sitting is required. Walking meditation is an ex-
cellent alternative. A beginner having difficulty can start with
five minutes of zazen and gradually increase the time. Even one
minute, or less, is a good place to begin, especially for children.
We need to remember that zazen starts with one breath at a time.
The main point is to allow the mind to learn to be quiet, to practice letting go of attachments.

Of course, we need to guard against becoming self-indulgent,
emphasizing comfort rather than practice. The cross-legged sitting posture provides exceptional balance of body and mind, enhancing deep, easy breathing. So we should encourage ourselves
and others to adopt this physical form as closely as we can, at the
same time understanding that getting there quickly is not the
point. Not everyone has the same capacity, not everyone can go
at the same pace. The point is simply to make our best effort.

deep roots

Buddha adjusted his teaching to each situation, including his students' abilities and temperaments and the circumstances. His teaching was specially blended in each case. Buddhism is well-known for its
capacity to adapt to the beliefs and cultures it encounters. But if Buddhism's teachings are continually adjusted, how is it possible to understand the fundamental teaching, the one that applies to every
person and every situation? The answer is, I think, that we need to adjust the teaching to current circumstances in order to fully understand it. The only way for us to appreciate the fundamental teaching
is to avoid clinging to a single way of teaching or a single way of expressing the truth.

Even though its expression must be flexible, truth itself never
changes. Because it is flexible, the teaching can express the truth. If
the teaching does not adapt, it cannot express the truth. Our practice

is the way of complete acceptance. We accept things as they are. We adjust and we adapt to circumstances and people. This is how we cultivate and express our deep mind.

When we deeply cultivate the soil, the roots of a plant have a place to go. Roots have to be buried in the soil because that is the nature of things that grow. When the roots are deep, the plant can thrive, even though leaves and fruit fall year after year. But if the roots are not deep, the plant cannot continue. When roots can go deep, full acceptance can take place, and everything can express itself according to its nature and circumstances.

In each relationship, we have to be aware of the nature of the person as well as the situation. However, they may not always be easy to distinguish. So we must continually keep our minds open and attentive. Full acceptance means that we are ready to respond according to each person and each activity. Like roots, we have to be able to go anywhere to find nourishment to support spiritual life. But "going anywhere" does not mean wandering aimlessly. The root travels far in many directions, but it does not leave the tree; it always knows what it is doing.

When we practice continuously, we can go anywhere and do anything, and always know what we are doing. When we know the true meaning of everyday activities, we can leave home but always feel at home. We have to start from home. This means that before we go anywhere, before we do anything, we should know what we are doing in a very big sense. We have to understand who we are to know what we are doing. That is why we sit. Inherently, everyone has a wide, accepting mind. Everyone has the power to respond according to a situation. Inherently we have unlimited, enlightened mind. But we have to make some effort to express it.

Zazen practice is how we express our wide, accepting mind. It is how we learn to express our true selves. When we have zazen practice, we can express ourselves completely. We have the confidence to go anywhere and never feel that we are away from home.

facing the world

To live according to the Zen way of life simply means to live completely. It means to be fully awake and engaged with the world in each moment, even when we are anxious and don't like the situation we are in. Someone who reads about zazen or who sees pictures of people sitting in the lotus posture may think, "That's not real life; they aren't doing anything." But zazen is not about taking a break from daily life. In zazen we are always ready to face the world, to be fully involved in it.

If we close our eyes, the darkness may provide us some relief from visual distraction and give us a feeling of peace and calm. But in zazen, we keep our eyes open. If we want to close our eyes because we feel distracted by what our eyes see, we need to understand that it is our minds that are distracted, not our eyes. So in zazen, we let our eyes remain open, aware, and ready. By keeping our eyes open, we stay in the world.

Instead of putting limits on our seeing, hearing, or thinking capacities, we should settle ourselves on the quiet that is inherent in the busyness and noisiness of daily life. It is necessary for us to face the world, to fully embrace it, so we can see it as it really is. Keeping our eyes open means that we do not create a false separation between ourselves and the world. Our emphasis is on both. When we do not separate ourselves from the world, Buddha is seeing the world. To keep our eyes open in zazen is to have Buddha's eyes.

In our form of Zen practice, we face the wall during zazen. Strictly speaking, people face the wall, but for Buddhas there is no wall; Buddhas face the entire world. In a practical sense, we say that we are facing the wall, but actually we are Buddha facing out, facing the world. Sitting alone or sitting together, we keep Buddha's eyes open so that we can face the world.

The greatest human mistake is to sacrifice the expression of our true selves for a small physical or emotional comfort. Our desire for a small comfort will only lead to a desire for a larger comfort, resulting in a feeling of separation from each other and the world. If we keep our eyes closed, then our ears, noses, tongues, bodies, and minds will be closed. Then we cannot enter the world, nor can the world enter us. We cannot see things as they are. Our lives are taken over by personal desires and emotions for the sake of a small, personal comfort. We shouldn't make this mistake.

We take care of our eyes, ears, noses, tongues, bodies, and minds with awareness of our breath. We start with our posture. Keeping our backs straight, our breath can come easily. Then our eyes, ears, noses tongues, bodies, and minds are open and ready. Zen practice is not ascetic, even though it may seem so when we have pain in our legs or backs or we feel very sleepy. In practice, we do not try to create discomfort. At the same time, we do not try to hold on to comfort, or wish we did not have discomfort. If we are comfortable, that's fine, but if we are not, that is also fine. The best thing to do is to find true comfort, which transcends how we happen to be feeling at the moment. Then we can share comfort with everyone. Then we can be in the world and the world can be in us.

If we close our eyes, if we try to ignore a difficulty that is facing us we may feel comfortable. But we cannot live life with our eyes closed. We have to be careful of having too much concern for our personal comfort. It will not bring us peace; it will only create more problems. Zazen is the expression of true comfort. It is our total being in the world. It is total seeing, hearing, and breathing the world. It is letting the world see, hear, and breathe us. With open eyes, ears, noses, tongues, bodies, and minds, we have confident posture. Then we can discover true comfort and have confidence in our lives.

an adventure

I met Suzuki-roshi at Haiku Zendo in late 1966, but I did not meet with him privately until the winter of the following year, when I attended my second one-day retreat. In mid-morning, someone announced that Suzuki-roshi would hold private interviews with anyone who would like to meet with him. Several of us proceeded to a dark hallway on the ground floor of the San Francisco Zen Center, outside the room where the interviews were taking place. We sat in meditation facing the wall, awaiting our turns. When I entered the room, I bowed in greeting as I had been instructed and sat cross-legged on the cushion facing Suzuki-roshi. He was patient and gentle, yet I was nervous about meeting a Zen master. Through the partially opened window behind him, I could hear the traffic on Bush Street. Unlike the hallway, the room was bright and cheerful. White, lacy curtains provided a gently flowing contrast to his dark robes and quiet, seated figure.

We sat in silence for several minutes, paying no attention to a long-legged spider that inched slowly up a side wall. Finally he said: "Do you have some question?" I answered: "No, I have no questions." After a long pause, he picked up a pad and pencil and asked for my name and address. He asked how the retreat was going. He said he recognized me from Haiku Zendo. Then we bowed to each other and I left.

Our second meeting took place at Haiku Zendo on a Thursday morning. We sat cross-legged in front of the large windows that had replaced the door of the former garage. Lowered blinds filtered the sunlight, bathing us in narrow, alternating stripes of light and shade. As I sat in the full lotus posture, soles turned upward, I realized that I had my bare feet practically in Suzuki-roshi's face. I made a mental note to wear socks next time. Again I had no questions. After a few minutes of sitting together in silence, he pointed to my folded legs and remarked: "You have good practice." Later I realized that even though I had no questions he had found a way to say something encouraging.

These first two meetings with Suzuki-roshi were disappointing. In those early days, influenced by the literature available, there was a widespread feeling that the purpose of Zen practice was to achieve an exciting enlightenment experience. I expected that he would give me instruction, a challenge, or a clue how to do it. But he didn't. He had no method other than simply paying attention and waiting to see what I had to say. His way was to allow me to discover things for myself. Finally I understood that I could not wait for him to take the lead. I should have something to talk about when I came to visit him privately.

One Wednesday evening, during the question-and-answer session following the weekly lecture, a young man asked Suzuki-roshi about a recent book that included a long section describing personal enlightenment experiences. The book was enormously popular. Many of us were pleased finally to have a glimpse of what the result of Zen practice was supposed to feel like. In response to the question, Suzuki-roshi said only, "There is some misunderstanding."

I was stunned. It was the closest thing to criticism that I could recall hearing from Suzuki-roshi. How could he be critical of such a wonderful and important book? I thought. Years later, I appreciated the intent of his remark. Suzuki-roshi did not encourage us to try to attain enlightenment; rather, he encouraged us to *express* enlightenment. The misunderstanding he referred to was in thinking that we had to *obtain* something. He said in later lectures, "Enlightenment is not some good feeling or some particular state of mind. The state of mind that exists when you sit in the right posture is, itself, enlightenment," and, "The points we emphasize are not the stage we attain, but the strong confidence we have in our original nature and the sincerity of our practice."[1]

For a long time, I didn't get it. The goal of Zen, I thought, was to get this enlightenment that I had read about. At a Thursday breakfast a few months after the Wednesday evening incident, with some frustration I said to Katagiri-roshi, "You never speak about enlightenment!" The breakfast table roared with laughter at his response: "Oh, don't you think so?" Only slowly did I begin to realize that there *is* no result, nothing to "get," from spiritual practice. Because it is selfless, practice *is* the end in itself.

Being with Suzuki-roshi informally was always delightful, often surprising. One evening, following a wedding ceremony at Haiku Zendo, we organized a celebration dinner in Marian's home. As we were sampling a variety of unusual delicacies, Suzuki-roshi picked up something exotic-looking and took a big bite. While he was chewing, I asked: "What is that you're eating? I've never seen it before." Without hesitation, he reached over, deposited the remaining portion in my mouth and said: "It's delicious. Why don't you try it?" It was lotus root, and it *was* delicious.

In the summer of 1967, shortly after it opened, Mary and I and our two children spent two weeks at Tassajara, the Zen monastery established by the San Francisco Zen Center in the Los Padres National Forest in central California. Mary is a landscape designer; one of her hobbies is cultivating bonsai trees. Suzuki-roshi also worked with bonsai and was developing a miniature rock garden behind his cabin at Tassajara. The two of them enjoyed talking about the care of bonsai.

One afternoon, Mary and I went for a hike. She took along a small shovel and some plastic bags, hoping to find some seedlings that she could plant at home. Alongside Tassajara Creek, she found a tiny oak that she liked. When we returned, she proudly showed her find to Suzuki-roshi. He promptly took it from her hands. He said, "Thank you very much," turned around, and went to his cabin without another word.

During the middle weekend of our two-week stay, several well-known Zen masters arrived from Japan to participate in a dedication ceremony for the new American monastery. They included Yasutani-roshi, Eido Tai Shimano-roshi, and Soen Nakagawa-roshi.[2] On Saturday morning, the Tassajara Zen students and summer guests gathered in the zendo for a dialogue with Suzuki-roshi and his special visitors. The four roshis and their assistants sat impressively on raised platforms in front of the altar. As the senior Yasutani-roshi delivered a lecture, translated by Eido-roshi.

Following the lecture, Richard Baker, one of Suzuki-roshi's senior students, announced that the audience could now ask questions of any of the four roshis. The room was silent. Dick encouraged us to speak up, pointing out our once-in-a-lifetime opportunity. Out of the sixty or seventy people in the zendo, I was the only one to raise a hand. I asked, "What is the best way to establish Zen in America?" The roshis and their attendants went into a huddle. Eido-roshi announced that all four of them would answer this question.

I cannot remember exactly what was said that morning. In dramatic fashion, the first three responses urged us to practice zazen with great determination, to attain enlightenment, and to establish meditation centers throughout the United States. As the host, Suzuki-roshi was the last to speak. When his turn came, he stood up, quietly said, "I have nothing to say," and walked out a side door. The zendo literally shook with our laughter as the session came to a surprisingly abrupt end.

When my alarm rang at 5:00 on a Saturday morning in June 1968, I rolled over in bed and decided not to go to Haiku Zendo. The early summer breeze was warm and fragrant. And there was my lovely wife lying beside me. I said to myself, "It's too nice to-day. You don't have to go." Then I thought of Marian, who was at that moment opening the meditation hall and preparing the rice, soup, and fruit for our breakfast. She didn't give herself the option of sleeping in. She was unselfishly making it possible for us to ex-perience Zen practice in suburban America. I quickly got out of bed and drove to Los Altos. That vision of Marian woke me up to selflessness. Since then, I never have difficulty getting out of bed for zazen at 5:00 A.M.

That morning, after the 9:00 meditation period, Marian called me aside. She explained that she could no longer afford to con-tinue living in her Los Altos home. Two of her four daughters had reached their twenty-first birthdays, ending child support from their father, her former husband. More important, Marian wanted to simplify her life. She wanted to go to Tassajara for monastic Zen practice. But she did not want to put an end to Haiku Zendo by selling the house. She told me, "I've wrestled with this problem for a year. When I saw you enter the zendo this morning, I knew I finally had my answer. Would you and your family consider mov-ing here and taking care of Haiku Zendo?"[3]

I was both startled by her question and pleased with the trust that she was willing to place in us. Later that morning, when I told Mary what had happened, she said, without hesitation, "If you want to do it, it's OK with me."

I struggled with Marian's invitation for several days, the chal-lenges we would face as well as the opportunity being offered. Many of our monthly expenses would double, as would the length of my daily commute to work. There were the administrative de-tails of maintaining Haiku Zendo, making sure that Saturday and Thursday breakfasts were prepared and that our visiting teacher was taken care of each week. The practical and economic consid-erations surrounding Marian's request flooded my mind. By con-trast, Mary simply saw it as an adventure.

The biggest concern we faced was Marian's two youngest daughters, who were still living at home, attending high school. Their father was remarried, living in another part of Los Altos. Marian felt strongly that the girls did not want to live with him. So we had to think seriously about becoming instant foster parents to two teenagers. At the time, our son, David, was six years old, and our daughter, Margaret, was three.

On the other hand, we were being given a chance to develop close relationships with two Zen masters who had come from Japan to establish Zen practice in America. Mary and I had great respect and fondness for both Suzuki-roshi and Katagiri-roshi. They exemplified strength of character, patience, humor, and a wisdom that was both down-to-earth and universal. Now we were being asked to help them. That's what decided it for me. My soul-searching about moving to Haiku Zendo confirmed my growing feeling that Zen practice encourages the best of human qualities and expresses something very fundamental about life.

So in September we moved into Marian's house, to be the caretakers of Haiku Zendo and Marian's daughters. We had to experiment a little bit to discover the best way for us to be with the girls. Mary recalled an incident that took place at the time:

> It occurred on the day we had an open house shortly after moving into Marian's house. Mrs. Suzuki and Roshi attended the party, as did many people, and the house was quite crowded. I was chatting with Roshi in the living room, when he asked me to get him a glass of water.
>
> He accompanied me to the kitchen, and when we were away from the crowd he said, "How do you feel about living here?" I think he wondered if I realized how much I was getting into. I answered that I was enthusiastic about all my new responsibilities, but that I did worry somewhat about Marian's teenage daughters, whom she left in our care. He

said, "Their behavior is beyond your control." That simple statement of fact gave me a new perspective in relating to the girls.[4]

Kathy and Annie were good-natured, independent, and self-sufficient. After some adjustment on everyone's part, living together really did become an adventure. The house always seemed to be full of the girls' high school friends or Zen students, sometimes both. I often had trouble figuring out who was who.

On a Wednesday evening in the fall of 1969, after everyone had departed Haiku Zendo, Mary, Katagiri-roshi, and I chatted as we put away the teacups. He surprised us by suggesting that Haiku Zendo might be ready for its own resident Zen teacher. Later, when the core group of Haiku Zendo expressed enthusiasm for the idea, I went to San Francisco to speak with Suzuki-roshi about it. He encouraged us, and he recommended that we invite the Zen monk Kobun Chino. Kobun was familiar to most of us.[5] Three years earlier, an American from San Francisco Zen Center had spent several months at Eiheiji, one of the two major training monasteries of the Soto Zen school in Japan.[6] He wrote to Suzuki-roshi, describing a young Japanese priest he had met and suggesting that he be invited to America. Marian and Suzuki-roshi invited Kobun to come to Haiku Zendo. But he didn't make it to Los Altos. When he arrived, Suzuki-roshi liked him so much that he immediately took him to Tassajara and installed him as assistant abbot. He stayed there for a year and a half, then returned to his home city of Kamo in central Japan to help repair his family temple, which had suffered damage in a flood.

Having already met Kobun, I was happy to invite him, once again, to be the resident teacher at Haiku Zendo. When he arrived in February 1970, my family took him into our home. It was natural that he should have the room used for so many years by

our weekly visitors from San Francisco. Even though activities at
Haiku Zendo took place just three times a week, he did not have
a great deal of free time once Zen students discovered that he was
available.

After I had been practicing for a little over a year, I started
meeting with Suzuki-roshi on a regular basis. I brought him many
questions about how Zen practice applied to contemporary American life and to my own life, particularly to my work environment.
He rarely gave specific advice but rather encouraged continuous
practice as the best way to resolve difficulties. During one of our
meetings, I described a particularly sensitive situation at work, in-
volving complex personal politics. "What do you think I should
do?" I asked. Ignoring my plea for him to solve my problem, he
simply said, "You have to go back to the source of your karma."

I didn't understand what he meant. I was puzzled by the Buddhist teaching about certain human activities creating karma, a
mysterious leftover negative energy that causes rebirth and suffering. But even though I would have preferred a more pragmatic response, I knew that he was trying to show me something. I was
intrigued by his answer, caught up in the uncertain meaning of
the terminology and its broad spiritual implications. I pondered
what it meant to "go back to the source."

I can't explain how it happened, but in time I understood
Suzuki-roshi's meaning. He was encouraging me to see how the
problem had been created. Rather than merely look for a solution,
I had to understand the process before trying to correct its end result. He was trying to help me see that I was bringing my own
habits, biases, and self-interests to the work situation. The problem was not just "out there"; I was part of it, I was creating it
through my own delusions. This was his way of saying that I had
to take a step backward before trying to go forward, that in order
to take care of the details of everyday life, I first had to recognize

desires and emotional patterns and how they cause difficulties to arise.

From a practical viewpoint, karma is a way of understanding the harmful consequences of our habits, those emotional, knee-jerk reactions to annoying or threatening situations that appear in life. Putting an end to these habits, and to the suffering they create, must start with recognizing their existence and accepting them as our own, as our problems, not somebody else's. All of this depends on unbiased, unfiltered awareness of what is going on.

Suzuki-roshi was gracious and easygoing. Yet at times he could become impatient, even angry, when he felt that people were stubbornly staying stuck in their delusions. A particularly memorable incident occurred toward the end of a one-week retreat at Zen Center's new location on Page Street. Hearing the wake-up bell, students dressed and started to proceed to the zendo when several realized that the bell had been struck one hour earlier than scheduled. Many returned to their rooms for more sleep, others went in search of a cup of tea, some continued on to the zendo. Following a second wake-up bell, after all students were seated facing the wall for the first zazen period of the day, Suzuki-roshi entered, carrying his *kyosaku*, a short teacher's staff, flattened at one end. He walked down the line of seated students, pausing behind each one to admonish the entire hall with a shout and deliver two blows to the shoulder: *"You don't know how to practice!"* (wap, wap); *"You don't know how to practice!"* (wap, wap).

By early 1970, I was irrevocably committed to the practice. Sitting in zazen first thing in the morning had become natural and spontaneous, the defining act of my day. An unmistaken vitality seemed to be missing if I didn't start the day that way. Even on business trips, I would take a pillow from the motel bed, wrap a blanket around myself, and sit for an hour before putting on my white shirt and suit and heading for breakfast in the coffee shop.

The form of the practice given to us by Suzuki-roshi—maintaining a single physical posture and keeping the mind alert by continuous awareness of the breath—is extraordinarily simple. Yet it is inexplicably profound. I found it impossible to explain with any precision what was going on. All I could say was that, in my own experience, zazen somehow encouraged confidence as well as generosity, patience, and caring through a subtly different way of seeing the world. I felt completely in accord with its non-dogmatic, themeless expression of universal spirituality. I had the feeling that I had come home.

In particular, I was encouraged by Zen's emphasis on discovering—or, perhaps more accurately, uncovering—inherent wisdom through one's own determination. Its fundamental spirit was characterized by Suzuki-roshi's primary emphasis on zazen, illustrated by the following incident. Suzuki-roshi arrived from Japan in 1959 at the invitation of the Japanese-American Zen Buddhist temple on Bush Street. A small group of Westerners found out about him and started a sitting group of twelve or so. One day, a young man from England, Grahame Petchey, arrived and, after morning zazen, said, "I am interested in learning about Zen. Can you teach me?"

Suzuki-roshi responded, "Come back tomorrow morning and I will explain." The next morning, he did not explain anything. After waiting three months, Grahame asked again, and Suzuki-roshi said, "We sit in the evening as well. Please come." He never did answer Grahame's question directly.[7]

I wanted to continue this spirit, to make this attitude the basis of my own practice, to be in the zendo every morning and to sit without expectation. This latter part, as it turned out, was not to be as easy as I supposed.

I started thinking about the future, about how I could continue to provide for others the practice I had discovered in the garage of a suburban home. I felt strongly about bringing together the best that America had to offer with this alive and compassionate spiritual practice. Eventually, I felt that Haiku Zendo would have to leave the comfort of a private home. It had to become more public, more accessible, so that interested people could feel a sense of ownership and learn to take care of it. But Kobun had recently arrived, and it was much too soon to talk about moving.

I began to think about becoming a Zen monk, one of Suzuki-roshi's disciples. As I had felt drawn closer to him during the previous two years, I became more and more aware of the depth of his effortless expression of patience and kindness. His quiet, natural way demonstrated that these are qualities inherent in everyone. I wanted to understand how he did it, to absorb his way of being in the world.

At the same time, I was aware of my limitations. I had serious doubts about my fitness to be one of Suzuki-roshi's disciples and possible successors. Emotionally, I was too logical, too impatient, plagued by a tendency to be critical. I was far from his quiet manner of total acceptance. How could I carry on his way, learn to express his selflessness, and be as encouraging to others as he was?

Was I sincere in my desire to become a monk or was it a scheme to gain self-esteem? Was I constructing a facade, an appearance, to cover up something about myself that I did not want to see? I became painfully aware that I *liked* the idea of *being known* as a monk, as one of Suzuki-roshi's students. The awareness made me feel unclean, as if I were sniffing the faint aroma of my own ego. I spoke to Kobun about my confusion. He just said, "You should go ahead."

Even with his encouragement, I remained skeptical. For several months, I struggled with my doubts, arguing with myself. "I'm too judgmental," I would say; "You'll get over it," I would respond. Little by little, I realized that I was being too self-critical, neglecting to trust both myself and the practice. Finally I started to understand that it was not necessary to be perfect. It was more important to continue to practice with determination, to try to be aware of self-oriented tendencies, to try not to allow them to poison circumstances or relationships. It meant proceeding with confidence, even if accompanied by uncertainty.

I didn't know what it meant to be a Zen monk in modern America. Nobody really did; the notion was still too new. I understood only that I wanted to be a monk while continuing to work and take care of my family, to develop an integrated, balanced life, expressing spiritual practice in the complexity of the everyday world. Was it possible to have the true spirit of a Zen monk while living a suburban, corporate life? Could I live in the world, fully involved, without seeking anything except how to live the authentic life?

In March of 1970, I made arrangements to meet with Suzuki-roshi to talk about becoming a monk—his student—in the Zen tradition, as well as to explain my doubts and reservations. As I drove to San Francisco on that cold, drizzly evening, the glare of oncoming traffic made the slick road difficult to see. The city was embraced by fog.

Suzuki-roshi was waiting for me in his small Zen Center apartment. It combined artifacts of two cultures. America provided glossy, enamel-white walls, a steam radiator with connecting pipes running along the baseboard, electrical outlets, and high sash windows. From Japan there were delicate statues, scrolls of elegant calligraphy, and mysterious Buddhist texts. The fragrance of incense lingered everywhere.

We sat on cushions next to the window overlooking Page Street. Suzuki-roshi poured me a cup of tea. I told him that I wanted to be his student. He asked me why I wanted to become a monk. As I started to explain, he immediately stood up and without a word went into an adjoining room. I sat alone with my teacup, looking out into the damp night, wondering what was next.

In a few minutes, he returned with his wife, known to everyone simply as Okusan.[8] She brought a measuring tape. They stood me up and held out my arms. Together they took my measurements: chest, waist, height, arm length. Then he said, "Your robes will arrive from Japan in six months. They will cost $150. Thank you for coming. Good night." I stepped into the dim second-floor hallway of Zen Center as he closed the door behind me. It was his way of saying, "Yes, you can become my disciple." He asked no further questions. I did not have a chance to explain.

So at the age of thirty-seven, I was going to become an American Zen monk, a disciple of a perceptive, down-to-earth, determined, unselfish Zen master. It was a rare opportunity that I was being given, a chance to bring together several worlds, to follow my intuition about the relationship of spirituality to everyday human activities. I wanted to understand how spirituality can be expressed at work, at home, and within social institutions. It was new territory; there were no instructions on how to proceed.

Suzuki-roshi gave no instructions either. It was up to me to determine what kind of Zen monk I was going to be. I decided that it was important to attend a three-month training period at Tassajara, to have some experience of monastic life. Mary encouraged me to do what I thought was best. She was willing to let me be gone from home for three months, to take care of the children, now eight and five years old, and to keep an administrative eye on Haiku Zendo. IBM granted me a leave of absence. I was impressed with the company's attitude, allowing one of its managers to take time off to attend a Zen monastery.

I spent the fall of 1970, from mid-September through mid-December, at Tassajara. Suzuki-roshi was in Japan taking care of business matters regarding his home temple. He had invited Tatsugami-roshi from Japan to act as abbot during his absence. Tatsugami-roshi was a large man. For fifteen years, he had been the *ino*, in charge of monks' conduct in the meditation hall, at Eiheiji monastery. He had firm ideas about providing discipline and organization to the fledgling monastery, staffed mostly by Americans who had grown up in the 1960s. He wanted us to learn the liturgy of the Japanese Soto Zen monastic tradition and had several people practice chanting five to six hours each day. On alternate evenings, in place of zazen, he would lecture for an hour and a half on Dogen's instructions for proper Zen monk behavior. It was not an entertaining topic. After a long, cold day, staying awake was a continuous challenge.

Winter at Tassajara was breathtaking—the roaring creek, the sharp-sided, steep mountains on either side of the narrow valley, yielding only narrow glimpses of the crystalline night sky, the mind-clearing sound of the morning bell, the dawn light slowly illuminating the silent, seated figures in the meditation hall. It was also wet and cold.

The cabins and dormitory rooms were not insulated. Storm windows consisted of plastic sheets tacked on wooden frames. The wind easily found its way through cracks in the walls. There was no heat outside the kitchen, except for the potbellied stove fired up in the dining room-cum-library during the one-hour morning study period. We looked forward to our bath at the end of the day, provided by Tassajara's legendary hot sulfur springs.

Trying to adjust to the austere way of life, I discovered how attached I was to the comforts of my middle-class home and lifestyle. Giving them up was not easy. At the beginning, feeling confined by the daily monastic life of meditation, manual labor, and study, my mind worked diligently at self-deception. Early in the practice period, I was eager to explain, to anyone, the importance of my work at IBM. How disappointing and how revealing to realize that nobody cared: the "importance" was my own invention. Slowly I became aware of the game. It was a profound experience to watch my mind persist in deceiving itself while it knew exactly what it was doing.

Several weeks passed before my noisy, confused mind settled down during zazen and work, allowing itself to be fully aware of the sounds of the birds, the wind in the trees, the roar of Tassajara Creek, and the endless stream of emotions. It was an intense monastic practice period. There was no place to hide from the delusions that presented themselves, no escape to warm comforts or entertaining distractions. Despite the difficulties, or more likely encouraged by them, it was a vital experience in understanding the nature of human desires and my own attachment to them.

My knees hurt, I ached all over, and, by December, my thumbs and the tips of my fingers remained frozen numb until midday. But, little by little, as my stubbornness softened, as my mind let go, it no longer fought the increasing cold and physical discomfort. What a great gift to realize that a pain in the knee does not have to become a pain in the mind, that the mind creates its own pain by refusing to accept the pain in the knee. One morning I became aware that my face had assumed a calm, slight smile during zazen. As mental images of myself faded from my mind, sitting became increasingly natural. Midway through the three months, a message came from San Francisco: my ordination ceremony was scheduled to take place in January, following Suzuki-roshi's return from Japan.

Almost fifty people crowded into Haiku Zendo that Saturday afternoon in 1971. My mother, living in San Francisco, arrived fifteen minutes after the ceremony had begun. She was nervous as she entered the packed room. Her middle-aged, middle-class son, with a nice family, nice job, nice home, and promising future, was preparing to become immersed in a mysterious religious world beyond her comprehension. She was certain that I was throwing away everything required for the "good life." She could not hide her anxiety. I can still see Suzuki-roshi's eyes glancing at her as she entered and took a seat someone offered her near the platform. Very gently, he reached over, put his hand on her shoulder, and said, "You have come just at the right time."

In September, I received a call from Zen Center asking me to come immediately to meet with Suzuki-roshi. I was asked to wear my monk's robes. He had been ill during the past year with flulike symptoms. On this bright, warm Sunday afternoon, I drove to San Francisco with apprehension. When I arrived at his room, he was in bed. He said to me, "I have cancer."

I was shaken. I asked him about an operation, and he said no treatment was possible. Then he asked: "Do you have a question?" Without thinking, I said: "Standing by the ocean, we see the crashing waves. From a distance, we see the calm, wide water itself." Closing his eyes and looking very tired, he said: "It is just so." He passed away in December.

CHAPTER 6

in reality

The nature of my work did not change when I returned from Tassajara. As if I had not been gone for three months, I slipped back into my job as manager of a systems analysis group. My monastic shaved head soon regained its crew cut. In my button-down shirts and wing-tip shoes, I was comfortably in place at IBM. Word got around. Many people knew where I had spent three months. A few expressed some interest in my involvement in Zen practice, but, in general, my working relationships picked up where they had left off.

Even though the work itself was essentially the same, my view of it had changed over the previous three years. Work had new contours. It no longer had a hard, "rocky" feeling, as if I were in an endless desert of problems to overcome and goals to attain, always in danger of stubbing my toe. Instead, work became like a garden, with new and interesting shapes, textures, and fragrances at each turn. Problems and difficulties did not go away, but my relationship with work was different. My new understanding of the meaning of success resulted in a change in priorities.

Working ceased to be a means to an end, for gaining recognition and a more comfortable life as quickly as possible. Success was now feeling satisfaction in the ongoing process of working, in the activity itself, in the taking care, not only in achieving goals. My primary interest shifted to the dynamic process of work, the best way of approaching tasks and relationships so that the work environment could express a spiritual, communal feeling. Concern for efficiency in each activity gave way to interest in the flowing nature of working. My workplace became my practice place. I was learning to take care of it the same way that I had learned to take care of Haiku Zendo.

learning satisfaction

In order for our lives to be happy, we need to know the meaning of true happiness, to understand that it is not based on material or emotional satisfactions. True happiness is based on appreciating our true selves. In other words, we need to know who we really are before we can have satisfactions, before our minds judge what "is" and what "is not" satisfying. Real happiness cannot be based on temporary satisfactions. It can only be based on understanding the original meaning of life.

A natural part of being human is to try to achieve a variety of satisfactions through the efforts of daily life. To have a spiritual life does not mean to deny these satisfactions. However, our main emphasis should be on our effort, not its results. The results of our effort come and go, but our effort is always here. So we should know what we are doing with our effort.

Our efforts are not just to obtain satisfactions. In other words, we should not reserve our so-called best effort for obtaining satisfactions and use so-called other efforts for nonsatisfying activities. If we do, our entire lives themselves will not be satisfying. When we have Zen practice, every activity is satisfying because all activities are beyond discrimination. To base our lives on spiritual practice means to emphasize our effort and not worry so much about attaining satisfaction. That is how all activities become satisfying. Then our entire lives are continuous feelings of satisfaction.

We know what we are doing with our effort when we see things as they really are. So we should try not to look at things in a limited way. Then we can see the original way of people and things and we can understand what we are doing with our lives. In Buddhism, to be awake means to understand what we are doing, even before we actually do something and even before we think of doing something. This understanding is the basis of our efforts.

Suzuki-roshi spoke about how we should "resume our way, our

original nature." He meant that we should be awake and not be caught by the discriminating mind. He also meant that we should have the Bodhisattva's mind, the compassionate mind that dedicates its efforts to others. But this dedication is not considered a self-sacrifice, because the Bodhisattva knows the true nature of satisfactions and that there is actually nothing to sacrifice. The Bodhisattva understands the true nature of her effort and that her life is a continuous "effortless effort." To the Bodhisattva, happiness and helping others are not different. In Buddhist literature, the idealized, dramatized Bodhisattva appears superhuman. But the true Bodhisattva is simply an individual who expresses her original nature. It is someone who practices with sincerity and makes an effort not to hold on to self-oriented ideas.

In zazen, we discover our own Bodhisattva minds. Practice means to be ready for that discovery. When we are ready to give up self-oriented ideas and to accept the true nature of things, we are truly Bodhisattvas. We just practice and let our own Bodhisattva natures appear.

We are all unique in our humanness, and we all express our ways differently. We have different interests and skills, so each one of us is satisfied by different activities. But the fact that we are unique does not mean that we are inherently different from each other. Our true nature is universal. Each one of us expresses the same true nature in our own unique way.

As experiences with work and with Zen multiplied, I began to recognize a variety of similarities between these two presumably different worlds of practice. Starting at the personal level, I saw that the being-in-the-world qualities emphasized in Zen were no different from the character traits that IBM encouraged in its people: integrity, morality, a capacity for work, self-discipline, willingness to learn, attention to detail, responsibility, and perseverance.

This recognition did not come as a great surprise. Rather, it was a verification of my instinct that these traditional American values were embodied in the long history of Zen Buddhism. I was excited about the creative possibilities of integrating the two traditions. I envisioned merging Buddhist compassion with the spirit of determination in the American way of life, a merger that would diminish the greed and injustice that seemed stubbornly to cling to the individualism inherent in our "pursuit of happiness."

Another similarity between work and Zen practice reflected the way people perceive the world they live and work in. Suzuki-roshi often spoke about seeing the world from the standpoint of Big Mind, what he sometimes called "vast mind" or "original mind," the mind that includes everything.[1] In the same way, work emphasizes "seeing the big picture" in the business or political sense.

Successful organizations require that customers, key managers, and other individuals review major proposals for new ventures to ensure that technical, financial, and personal impacts are well understood. In order to respond to what often turns out to be intense scrutiny, whoever originates a project must recognize the wide range of positive and negative consequences that could result from his or her proposed change. What is fondly known as "doing your homework" depends on including everything, developing an awareness of the total business, technical, or political situation rather than confining attention to a limited area of interest.

The activities of the individual as well as those of the entire organization require this big-picture discipline in order to avoid problems that could undermine a project. It is needed to reduce the possibility of problems occurring after the proposed change is implemented. Seeing the big picture—the entire process—is the best way to avoid "business karma."

At first, developing the big picture and developing Big Mind may not seem to have much in common. Seeing the big picture is a conscious, logical process, required in innovative, complex, or

changing environments. Big Mind, by contrast, is not imposed by
an institution or by society. It is a wide-view, spiritual perspective
that develops naturally from continued mindfulness of one's total
world of experience. Its basis is compassion, rather than return on
investment. But these two ways of seeing—one by relying on
analytical thinking, the other by setting it aside—share important
features. They both require personal determination to develop
as much understanding as possible, as well as willingness to
acknowledge—not ignore, deny, or diminish—whatever is discovered. In my own experience, the business attitude and the spiritual attitude do not conflict but rather complement each other.

    In my experiences with discouragement, I noticed a third simi-
larity between work and Zen practice. When I started work I had
no idea of the difficulties that could arise, never imagining that I
would encounter serious doubts and concerns. I was in a dream-
world then, naive and eager because of having made it through a
rigorous college program, receiving the industry's attention as a
young engineer, settling in the San Francisco Bay area, and experiencing the optimism and opportunity at IBM. But in less than a
month on the job testing RAMACs, and later as an engineer and
in sales, I came face to face with discouragement, anxiety, and
doubt.
    With great relief, I realized that these emotions arose in pro-
portion to the pride I felt in what I had previously accomplished
and in my assumptions about what the future was supposed to
bring. I learned that I had to examine the source of each disappointing situation and figure out how to be as creative as possible in it. They were lessons in the risks associated with high
expectations, the wisdom of not trying to create the future in
advance, and the value of simply being ready for whatever might
occur.
    As counterpoints to what happened on the job, two experi-

ences of discouragement associated with my Zen practice stand out. The first developed through my relationship with Kobun Chino. After living with my family for nearly a year, Kobun married a young woman he had met when he was at Tassajara. They moved into a house nearby. He was firmly established as the teacher at Haiku Zendo and was developing a reputation in California and beyond. Many people were attracted to him both as a teacher and as a friend. He was intuitive, gentle, warm, generous, knowledgeable, and full of good humor. He was the spiritual leader for a large number of people who practiced at Haiku Zendo as well as for many he had met elsewhere.

When Suzuki-roshi passed away, I assumed that Kobun was to become my Zen mentor. I was looking forward to developing our relationship further. In traditional Zen practice, this relationship between teacher and student is the essential component of training and of teaching. For a Zen monk, frequent meetings with the teacher are absolutely fundamental. Arranging to meet with Suzuki-roshi was never easy because of our busy schedules and the geographic distance between us. Yet I was fortunate to meet with him enough to feel a growing intimacy. I planned to meet often with Kobun. It would be an easy matter, I thought, because he lived just around the corner.

It was not as simple as I had supposed. Kobun was hard to pin down. Because of the number of people who wanted to see him and my own busy work and family life, we had to schedule our meetings two weeks or so in advance. He often canceled at the last minute. When we did meet, he would allow himself to be called away by a visitor or telephone call, and our time together would end abruptly. It would then take an additional two weeks to schedule another meeting, with the same results. Sometimes he would forget about our appointment altogether.

I was angered and disappointed by Kobun's indifference, upset at his lack of consideration. After all, I thought, it was mostly through my efforts and those of my family that he had been given the opportunity to establish himself in America. And I was conscientiously taking care of Haiku Zendo, making it possible for him to give public lectures and for people to come in contact with him and with the practice. My discouragement continued for months.

Very slowly, though, that feeling changed. Gradually I realized that I had created the difficulty myself by expecting, and insisting on, a certain kind of relationship with Kobun. When it didn't work out the way I assumed it was supposed to, I blamed him, not stopping to consider that perhaps he had a totally different expectation, or maybe even none at all. Whether my anger was "justified" or not by Kobun's behavior toward me, I began to understand that I was actually *choosing* to be angry and that I was foolish to want to change him or expect him to be something he was not. I gave up worrying about what I felt was his indifference. Rather than dwell on the difficulties of the relationship, I learned to emphasize the positive ways that we could be together.

So I stopped trying to visit with Kobun, to have a special, personal teacher-student relationship. I accepted the ambiguity of our association. With continued practice, my attitude toward relationships changed. My intellectual understanding of the importance of establishing and maintaining good relationships had not prevented me from being blinded by my own desires and expectations of other people. Finally recognizing my tendency, I was able to accept the reality of my relationship with Kobun. I was learning how disappointment and discouragement arise and to understand what it means to express the unattached mindfulness of spiritual practice in everyday life.

One incident that helped me appreciate my relationship with Kobun occurred a few years after he arrived at Haiku Zendo. During the 1970s, a small radio station in Los Gatos broadcast a fifteen-minute religious program on Sunday evenings. I was invited to appear and asked Kobun to join me. Midway through the program, the moderator asked me, "What techniques do you use to encourage people in their meditation practice?" With some pride, I said that we did not use special techniques, such as visualizations, enigmatic riddles, promises of spiritual attainment, or strict discipline.

Kobun then spoke up. He said, "We use the most important technique—people's own sincerity." Hearing his words, I was staggered, as if I had been struck by an icy ocean wave. My spine tingled; I began to perspire. I felt numb and giddy as my mind seemed to float and expand. His few words went directly to the heart of spiritual understanding, cutting through the analytic limitations of my own rational answer.

My second memorable encounter with discouragement in Zen practice took place in 1973, when I returned to Tassajara for a second training period, this time as head monk, or *shuso*. Following the traditional monastic tradition, I was chronologically the next of Suzuki-roshi's disciples to be shuso. Again, IBM granted me a three-month leave of absence. In traditional Zen monasteries, the head monk is expected to provide the model of behavior for the other monks and to act as spiritual leader in the absence of the abbot.

Many of the students at Tassajara were skeptical about what I was doing there. Several were antagonistic. There was a feeling that I was not an authentic Zen student, and certainly not a legitimate monk, since I worked for a large corporation and lived a middle-class life. During a question-and-answer period following one of my lectures, a young man shouted: "How can you work for that rip-off company?"

I don't believe his anger was aimed specifically at IBM. I think he was expressing a general frustration with large organizations that are indifferent, and sometimes abusive, to people and to the environment. Maybe he saw me as part of that power structure. At the time, most of the students at Tassajara were in their twenties. I was forty. Perhaps the age difference and cultural gap made me a natural target of their concern about the lack of personal, communal feeling in American institutions. Ironically, I felt the same way they did. After an initial period of disappointment with their indifference, I recognized that I could actually choose *not* to be discouraged by their misunderstanding of my intentions. By simply focusing on why I was there, I practiced putting the discouragement aside. It was the same "technique" I had used when I prospected for IBM.

Years later, I attended a Tassajara reunion at which several people apologized for their behavior that winter. As one woman explained, "You were doing then what we are trying to do now." She was talking about finding the balance, expressing spirituality while establishing a career and family.

It may seem strange, but I recall these experiences of discouragement with a sense of gratitude rather than of failure. For it was in these painful times of confusion and doubt that I saw how the mind creates problems and learned the meaning of determination and mindfulness.

the myth of progress

Many people who try zazen do not continue for very long, usually because they feel stuck. They detect no change in themselves, no progress in becoming a "better" person or achieving some ideal that they have in mind. I remember my own frustration with stubborn habits that did not seem to go away. My impatience with zazen receded when I finally recognized that spiritual practice is not to be measured by speed or efficiency and that my desire for progress was just one more desire.

If we find ourselves discouraged by lack of spiritual progress, after several weeks, months, even years, we do not need to be concerned that our practice is somehow not working. Actually, when we become aware that we feel discouraged, we should allow ourselves to be *encouraged* by the stick-to-it effort we have made up to that moment. Our continuous effort is a reflection of our sincerity and determination. It shows that we have a deep feeling about our lives and that we have maintained our practice without turning away from uncertainty. That continuation itself is the only real measure of progress we need.

We all want to feel encouragement, a marvelous antidote for doubt and anxiety. We don't like to feel that we are wasting our time; we want unambiguous, positive acknowledgment of ourselves and our efforts. So it is natural that we hope for greater intellectual understanding and deeper intuitive revelations in our spiritual practice, indications of progress that satisfy our thinking minds, our thirst for rational certainty.

But if we sense a new understanding or insight in ourselves, we have to be careful not to become proud of what we think we have attained. Our pride will create self-satisfaction, threatening our determination. By starting to emphasize attainment, we become less patient and more susceptible to discouragement. So if we think that we have attained something, it is important for us not to think about it too much or try to hold on to the exciting feeling it gives us. The best thing that we can do is just resume our attitude that is ready for anything, including the possibility of discouragement.

Modern society emphasizes progress and achievement in the day-to-day affairs of life. But to anticipate progress in spiritual practice is a misunderstanding. It is not necessary to be concerned about a spiritual report card. If we feel that we need to measure spiritual progress, it is because we do not yet understand that our spirituality is already complete. Zazen is not concerned about progress; it is simply the expression of our inherent completeness.

So no matter how we may feel, we just continue our practice. If we feel encouraged, we notice our feeling and continue. Or if we feel discouraged, we notice it and continue. This attitude is reflected in the well-known Zen story of "Hot Buddha, Cold Buddha," associated with Tozan, one of the founders of the Soto Zen school in ninth-century China.

According to this story, a monk asked Tozan: "In winter, it is very cold. In summer, it is very hot. How can we avoid them?"

Tozan said to him: "Why don't you go where there is no cold or heat?"

The monk asked: "Where is the place where there is no cold or heat?"

Tozan replied: "When cold, be cold Buddha, when hot, be hot Buddha."

This story illustrates the down-to-earth spirit of Zen practice. It means that when we feel encouraged, we are "Encouraged Buddha" and when we feel discouraged, we are "Discouraged Buddha." Tozan tells us that no matter how comfortable or uncomfortable we may feel, we never stop being Buddha.

We cannot always expect to be 100 percent comfortable. The world around us changes. Very rarely can we know what to expect. We just prepare as completely as we can and go ahead. When our minds are not attached to preconceived notions of how things should be, they can take care of anything that arises. Then we are ready to accept discomfort and not be discouraged by it. Zen practice is how we respond to the unexpected and appreciate the constantly changing world.

Discouragement results when our minds dwell on past disappointments, expectations that were not met. When we are aware of its source, we can actually use our discouragement as a signal to become awake to something that we are carrying around in our minds, something that is affecting our attitude toward our work. Practice enables us to change discouragement from something negative to something positive.

from disappointment to determination

When we really set our minds to do something, we do not allow ourselves to be deterred by difficulties or disappointments. It makes no difference if we are working on a scientific, academic, business, political, community, or family activity. It makes no difference if the difficulty comes from disagreement with another person or a change in the situation that we could not anticipate. When we truly want to get something done, we just keep seeking new ways to complete the task, some new relationship that works. When we are motivated, we keep trying even if we feel disappointed.

Determination to follow through is vital if we want to live our lives according to a vision or purpose that we believe in. Our effort has to be uninterrupted. We cannot allow ourselves to be stopped by disappointments. Disappointments occur when we have expectations that are not fulfilled. Sometimes expectations arise because something in our lives or in society has been a particular way for a long time and we assume that it will continue without change. Or we may have expectations when we make an arrangement with others, relying on them to keep their promise to do something. Having expectations is very natural.

If we frequently feel disappointment because our expectations are not met, it may mean that we are out of touch with the way things go in life, that we do not accept the truth that circumstances and people change, even things and people that have always been predictable. If we take our disappointments personally and feel that they are our fault or that we are being rejected by someone, then they will be very troublesome. We have to know what to do when disappointment appears.

So we practice awareness of ordinary, every-moment occurrences. We practice awareness of the activities of our minds and of our minds' responses to the changing world.

We practice giving the gift of acknowledgment to the activities of our own minds. We invite them home; we do not cut them off. Then we can give the same gift to the minds of others. We can invite them home by listening and acknowledging.

We do not try to transcend our human nature with our practice, nor do we strive toward some idea of perfection. Even when we feel disappointment, we continue to encourage the complete expression of life's activity moment by moment, in the midst of human imperfections. Our determination is how we express our inherent perfection, how we give the gift of inherent perfection to others.

finding the balance

Life can be very confusing. When it is, it can also be very painful. So naturally in our everyday lives we try to prevent confusion and to end it quickly when it arises. In addition, we often try to ignore confusion. However, in Zen practice, we don't ignore confusion when it appears; we actually welcome it. When confusion arises in our practice, it means that we have discovered something new. The feeling of confusion is an indication that we are trying to understand something. So welcoming confusion is actually an expression of wisdom. But before we can welcome it and be prepared to face it we have to know its nature.

Sometimes we are confused about the relationship of things, events, and people in our relative, everyday lives. Sometimes we are confused about the nature of Absolute Reality, which transcends everyday life. We need to resolve both kinds of confusion. We cannot truly relieve the confusion that appears in our everyday lives if we are confused about Absolute Reality. And we cannot understand the nature of Absolute Reality if we are not willing to address confusion that appears in our everyday lives.

As human beings, we have developed a variety of religious beliefs and philosophies to help us eliminate confusion about Absolute Reality. We have tried to establish various systems of thought that will provide something substantial to grasp, intellectually or emotionally. These beliefs are like hand straps in a subway or bus, something that we can hang on to so that we won't fall down.

In our everyday lives, we use our intellects to eliminate confusion. Rationally, we solve problems, we fix things, we organize our life situations. So naturally we believe that we can use our intellects, our everyday problem solvers, to eliminate any confusion we have about Absolute Reality. But our misunderstanding about Absolute Reality was created by our intellects. When we are impressed with an idea that we hear or read or resolve in our own minds, we accept it. Then wanting to believe what we have intellectually accepted, we become attached to it, we make an emotional investment in it. In other words, we create a hand strap for our minds.

When we were kids, my friends and I liked to stand up on the New York subway without holding on. We did it to test our skill at balance, while the train lurched and changed speeds. It required us to pay attention and quickly adjust our balance.

Passengers on a moving train or bus hold on to hand straps for safety. Holding on to an idea or belief can also help us feel safe by providing relief from confusion. But unnecessarily clinging to ideas and beliefs is a form of delusion. Such clinging closes the mind and prevents it from seeing something new. So when it comes to understanding Absolute Reality, we have to let go of our attachments, our beliefs, and our intellects. We have to let go of the strap and find our natural balance in every moment.

Relieving confusion in our relative, daily lives is hard work. We have to study situations, make choices, take risks, make mistakes, evaluate and remember the experience, sometimes stop what we are doing and try another way. And we have to be ready to face new, baffling situations. They arise continually just because we are alive. It is the same for all creatures. When we face the confusion of everyday life with determination, rather than ignore it, we are gaining experience to handle the next situation. We are training ourselves to face whatever appears.

Relieving the confusion about Absolute Reality is also hard work, but not for the same reason. We cannot use our intellects to understand Absolute Reality. Instead, we have to let intellect go. But it is not easy to put aside intellect and ego. We will only look for ways to end our confusion about Absolute Reality when we admit that stubborn clinging to ideas does not work.

Dogen wrote that we should "establish practice in the midst of delusion." He meant that we start to practice when we feel confused about Absolute Reality, when we feel off balance. At first, we think that we need a hand strap to keep our balance. But through practice we learn that we must give up the strap so that we can find our own inherent balance. In other words, we have to live in the midst of our confusion if we are to resolve it. We cannot simply apply preestablished beliefs to some new discovery, some new confusion. Giving up the strap is difficult; we resist it. Our minds can be very stubborn about letting go of a cherished belief.

Giving up the hand strap is how we find our balance, our confidence. When we are in balance, there is no confusion about Reality. When we keep our spiritual balance in everyday life, its confusions prove not to be confusions at all. Spiritual balance means facing new situations with confidence. It means welcoming confusion.

relationships

A fourth similarity between work and Zen practice emerged as I realized that almost everything I did on the job took place within a set of relationships. Even working alone, I sensed that none of my activities was ever dissociated from other people and what they were doing. Through an unspoken mutual sense of purpose, our efforts were related. Constantly evolving webs of relationships existed within the larger organization. I felt that this feature of corporate life, of the working world, reflected the Buddhist understanding of the inherent interconnectedness of all things.

I gained an appreciation for the importance of relationships at work during a dialogue that had taken place in one of my MBA classes at Santa Clara University. Our professor, Dr. Lawrence Lockley, asked the marketing class, "What is the primary purpose of a business?" We offered a variety of answers, financial and social:

"To make a profit."

"To provide an adequate return on investment to the owners."

"To provide useful goods or services."

"To create jobs."

Dr. Lockley nodded acknowledgment to each response. But he made no comment. By the end of the hour, the class had not found the answer that he wanted. We took up the question the following week. Again, he acknowledged but did not evaluate our responses. We admired our knowledgeable, inspiring, and warm-hearted teacher, who was, in addition, a well-respected economist whose views were published in a monthly newsletter. So we were groping, searching for the answer that would generate a favorable reaction. When we finally ran out of possibilities, he told us simply, "The purpose of a business is to survive."

His remark raised eyebrows, implying that a business has the same fundamental instincts as all living things. In the discussion that followed, we reflected on how a business organization must concern itself with the ongoing process of staying alive, just like any person, plant, or animal. We considered several aspects of this philosophy.

Perhaps the most important was the recognition that a business must remain flexible enough to adapt to changing conditions in its environment. There was no disagreement about the perils of not recognizing change or refusing to adapt to new economic or business circumstances.

From a primitive standpoint, the survival view of a business implies that an organization faced with failure might resort to painful activities, such as layoffs, and even consider predatory, unethical behaviors in order to avoid extinction. The emotional intensity of the class rose incrementally as we argued and explored the public and social responsibilities of a business enterprise.

Survival also means that a business requires a long-range vision, emphasizing continuity into the future rather than limiting itself to short-term objectives. So we talked about setting aside the desire for quick profits in order to invest in the long run. Years later I recognized this view as being consistent with the emphasis that Zen places on the continuous, never-ending nature of spiritual practice rather than on a one-time personal goal.

We discussed how the survival of any organism depends on its good health, and how the health of an organization, in turn, depends on continuously nurturing its relationships—customers, suppliers, the people who work together, even competitors and government agencies. We also considered an organization's need to take care of the resources that sustain it, to avoid overusing or polluting such resources, to maintain their balance, if the organization is to survive. Our academic discussion, which began with an exploration of business objectives, reinforced my own work experience of the need to understand, relate to, and continuously take care of the environment that supports work and life.

a matter of trust: a story

I arrived at work on a Monday morning to find a colleague, wearing a very serious look, waiting in my office. Mike and I had worked together on several projects over the years. We had always gotten along well. "Can you help me with a problem?" he asked. "It's been bothering me all weekend."

The time was the late 1960s, many years before the appearance of on-line terminals, personal computers, and workstations. The pervasive punch card was still a primary method for entering data in computers and accounting machines. Many administrative applications—reports, graphs, numerical analyses—were still being done with typewriters and calculators. The group that I managed acted as consultants, problem solvers, and troubleshooters. We supported the technical and administrative departments of the IBM San Jose product development laboratory by creating new and improved procedures for gathering, processing, and analyzing business and financial information. Mike had come to the right place for help.

Mike had been asked to provide his manager with additional inventory control information. He described the complicated method that he presently used to keep inventory records for his engineering group. He did not see how his current system, using cards, hand calculations, and typed reports, could provide the new information without a great deal of difficulty.

Mike's request was informal, between friends; we agreed that we didn't need to make a big project out of it. I worked on his problem on and off over the next few days. By the end of the week, I had worked out a reasonable solution. I explained it to him and gave him my handwritten notes and some diagrams. "Should I have this typed up?" I asked.

"Heck, no, I can read this," he answered. "It's just for my own use."

Several months later, I learned by accident that Mike had implemented the new procedure I had given him and then applied for, and received, a cash award from IBM. From my notes, he had prepared a written proposal, made a presentation to his management, and been given several hundred dollars, based on an estimated cost savings of several thousand dollars.

I was furious. Without saying a word, Mike had developed a formal procedure from my notes, claiming it as his own work. Money was not the issue. I was angry because Mike had betrayed my trust, secretly using my help for his personal advantage. I was upset that money and ambition were more important to him than our working relationship. Instead of being grateful for my help, he repaid me with deception.

I wanted revenge. Just the thought of getting even made me feel better. I pictured him embarrassed, exposed as a cheat, and chastened by IBM for dishonesty. Over the next few days, I considered how I could retaliate. I did not tell anyone else what had happened. But then my intense feelings started to diminish and I began to have doubts about my anger. Troubling questions formed in my mind: "What do you hope to accomplish by revenge? What does getting even really mean to you?"

The questions would not go away. I tried to convince myself that my indignation was justified, but the nagging persisted, forcing me to face my emotions and motives. What I really wanted, I eventually realized, was to see Mike hurt so that I could be relieved of my own hurt. I wanted to transfer my suffering to him.

I explored my hurt feelings. Was I really suffering? Who was actually hurt? I *felt* like I was suffering: there was anger and there was pain. Yet when I looked closely at what was really hurt, the only bruise that I could find was to my ego. I saw Mike's deception as a cynical way of saying, "You aren't really my friend, so I can take advantage of you." But my bruised mental image—made up of desires, memories, and fantasies—had no tangible reality, so nothing was really hurt or even threatened. If I was suffering, it was because I was allowing myself to be captive to my ego's precious image of itself. I was actually choosing to suffer! As this understanding became clear, the cloud of anger evaporated.

Thinking more rationally, I recognized that trying to expose what Mike had done would only create stubbornness and bad feelings. If I "got even" with him, he would probably want to "get even" with me. We would have a very difficult time working together in the future.

I realized that getting even doesn't really work. Throughout history, families, societies, and nations have used revenge as a means to establish "justice," but it has led only to war and additional suffering. Getting even does not make things even; one side is always the conqueror, the other side, the conquered. Following a confrontation, there is always a winner and a loser.

Arriving at this intellectual understanding of the futility of getting even was not, however, enough for me. I felt that I had to do something, to find a creative way to respond to the dishonesty, not for myself but for everyone, because if abuse is allowed to persist, it destroys community as well as individuals. Since it was impossible to fix the past, like replacing a broken window or patching a hole in the wall, I thought instead about the future. I went to see Mike.

I found him in his office. He stood up, extending his hand to greet me, the heels of his cowboy boots striking a curiously hollow sound on the corporate linoleum. With an enthusiastic smile, he exclaimed, "Hey, buddy, haven't seen you in a while. Come on in. How you doing?"

"I'm doing well, Mike. How are you?" I answered.

Along with boxes of punch cards and computer printouts, a variety of mechanical parts and subassemblies crowded his office. Mike was definitely a hardware person. He was proud of his foreign car, with the oversized engine that left virtually no space under the hood. The need to remove the fire wall to replace the number four and eight spark plugs added to his pleasure of ownership. He had a photo of the car on the wall over his desk. He was smoking a Marca Petri, one of those small, delicious, black Italian cigars. I accepted his offer to join him as he held out the open box.

"Say, Mike, when are you going to take me for a spin?" I began.

"Anytime. You name it."

"Great. How about one day next week during lunch?"

"Just let me know when."

"I will. Listen, I wanted to talk to you about something," I said as I lit up. "I heard that you got an award for that inventory procedure we spoke about some time ago."

"Yeah, I did," he answered.

"Well," I said, "I don't think you should have applied for an award."

"How come?"

"Because you really didn't solve that problem. Applying for an award gives the impression that you did. I don't think it's right to pass off somebody else's work as your own."

"As far as I'm concerned, we worked on that together, and I'm entitled to what I got. You sound as if I took advantage of you."

"You know, at first I thought so. I was steaming mad at you for taking credit for my work, after I had done you a favor. I was so angry that I started thinking of ways to get even. But you're right. Personally, I didn't lose a thing. It's just that I thought we were friends, and you went behind my back. I wish you would have told me what you had in mind. It's a matter of trust. I might not have liked it, but at least you would have been honest with me."

"You're imagining things." Mike was getting angry. "I didn't go behind your back. I was entitled to the award."

I didn't want to prolong the discussion, but I still had one more point to make: "That may be the way that you feel, but I don't. Anyway, I don't want to argue about it. I just want you to know that I would appreciate it if you would be completely honest with me when we work together again."

I thanked him for the cigar as I left.

Maybe Mike really believed that his actions had been totally aboveboard. Or, maybe he knew exactly what he had done and was being defensive. Whatever the case, I didn't feel there was anything to gain by debating. I simply wanted to let him know how I felt and what I would like in the future. We never did work together again, so I don't know if our conversation made any difference.

Despite my initial angry feelings, zazen practice enabled my mind to be flexible and open enough to accept a new way of seeing the situation. I could recognize my own misconception about revenge and question my anger and the value of getting even. Without practice, pride and stubbornness might have caused me to create an ugly situation out of one that was merely emotionally uncomfortable. I might still be harboring ill feelings today.

The Dalai Lama encourages the people of Tibet not to hate their Chinese conquerors. Instead, he advocates treating them with kindness. What a radical idea, not to harbor ill will toward your oppressor! Why would he say such a thing? It is because he knows that the desire for revenge remains a burden throughout an individual's life and is passed on to future generations as well, creating more suffering, manifesting what Buddhists mean by karma. Perhaps this is why greed, anger, and delusion are known in Buddhism as the three poisons.

no cutting off

When we feel disappointed by what someone says or does, we have to be careful not to cut off our relationship with her. We should try to take care of the relationship by setting aside our personal feelings of disappointment or hurt. The relationship is more important than the broken promise or how we feel, so we have to simply try again to complete the task.

If we feel disappointment, it doesn't help to say, "What a fool he is!" When we are not blinded by our expectations, we have a chance to look at a broken promise and consider: "Maybe it wasn't possible to do it the way we originally agreed." And we can allow ourselves to think, "How can I help make it possible?" With that kind of understanding, we can create a new way to complete the task and find a new approach to our relationship. The worst thing that we can do is create separation because of our disappointment. In other words, we shouldn't perform unnecessary surgery on relationships that feel troublesome. We should continue our practice by staying aware of our emotions and of our minds' reactions to disappointment. In that way, we can understand the tendencies of our minds and how they like to perform surgery.

If we continually have difficulty with someone, it is a misunderstanding to try to change that person. It is better to recognize and emphasize what is pure and creative in her, and to encourage it through our awareness and acceptance. This isn't always so simple because we can easily get caught in the emotions and fears of other people. We get caught because of our own fears, because our minds are not empty and ready. We get caught by our own self-oriented notions and delusions.

In our spiritual practice, we are not striving to transcend our human nature. We are simply trying to remain aware of the activities of our minds and how our lives are going. When emotions or desires appear in our minds, we acknowledge them and accept that they appear simply because we are human. We cannot prevent them from appearing, so we don't even try. Our practice is about not getting caught by them, because we understand how they get in the way of relationships.

finding our fit

The most important concern of our lives is our relationships with each other. Only when we have harmonious relationships can we have freedom. By emphasizing relationships we free ourselves from the notion of a small self and we avoid creating imaginary boundaries between ourselves and others. Through harmonious relationships we express our unlimited selves. This is the best way to find true satisfaction in life.

We become indifferent to relationships when our orientation is mainly toward ourselves, causing us to turn our faces and minds away from people when we do not get what we want from them. We cannot find true satisfaction with this attitude. To be indifferent with our lives is a big mistake. Instead, our practice is to pay careful attention to each relationship.

Creating harmonious relationships means taking care of and having a nurturing attitude toward everyone and everything. Recognizing that every relationship is precious gives us the determination not to create boundaries between ourselves and others. With this understanding, we are always ready to let go of our personal notions.

Creating harmonious relationships often requires us to adjust how we interact with each other. We do not always "fit" together, like pre-cut pieces of a jigsaw puzzle or a carefully hand-crafted box and lid. In some areas of our relationship we may fit, but in others we may not fit. Our practice includes recognizing these differences. If we don't, we will have friction and difficulties in our relationships. We have continuous trouble with our areas of "no fit" when our minds are attached to some fixed idea about what we should have or how things should be. So if we feel friction with others, the best thing to do is explore our own expectations of them. Continually placing stubborn demands on people cannot create harmony.

In Zen practice we let our minds be as fluid as water. Then they naturally assume their fit with everything. Whether water is moving quickly or being still, it always "fits" with its surroundings. There is no way to detect a separation between water and its surroundings.

We often let our minds fill up with personal concerns. When that happens, our minds lose their fluid feeling. They resist "taking in" another concern, especially someone else's problem. So we resist seeing or listening to others because we do not want to let them into our crowded minds. Rather than being like water, our minds become as hard as a stone. Then, like islands, we feel isolated, surrounded by hostility and the threat of invasion. And we think that we need to stock up on material and emotional possessions in order to defend our islands against siege.

If we let our minds become well-defended islands, we may feel secure but we will also feel captive. We cannot feel freedom if we are always defending our islands against others. Freedom is understanding that inherently there are no islands. It is understanding that there are no boundaries between ourselves and others. Our inherent freedom is expressed through harmonious relationships.

Expressing spirituality is not a sign of weakness. On the contrary, it is expressing our understanding. It means that we know who we are and that we have confidence in our lives. Spirituality is our fluid minds expressing themselves. When this happens it is easy to have harmonious relationships.

Spiritual practice is our effort to keep our minds ready, empty of personal concerns. To be empty of personal concerns does not mean that we do not take care of the details of our daily lives. It simply means that we do not create artificial boundaries with other people. We simultaneously take care of ourselves and each other. So when we empty our own minds, we are actually helping other people to empty their minds.

Recognizing areas of no fit, we naturally adjust ourselves to others. Then when we respond to them and are willing to let them in we are actually encouraging them. And we are inviting them to do the same. Our practice encourages us not to turn away from people who we feel are difficult or who do not give us what we want. Zen practice is one continuous effort to find our fit with each other.

Most businesses avoid association with any particular religion. However, this wise policy does not mean that we need to be afraid to express our spirituality at work, only that we have to understand what this expression really means. It is not voicing personal religious convictions. It is demonstrating our understanding of the sanctity of all things, in the way we take care of relationships and tasks.

At work, we don't speak philosophically about "supernatural power and marvelous activity." We use the language of "drawing water and carrying firewood," of the everyday activities of getting the job done: planning, sweeping, designing, cooking, selling, writing, serving, coding, painting, assembling, testing, negotiating, teaching, problem solving, truck loading. The expression of spiritual practice appears in the guise of these ordinary, everyday activities.

garden of emptiness

Out of the relationships of things and people, something new appears. The world is very dull if we only see things separately, such as the moon without clouds, mountains without sky, or people without each other. If we look at a tree, or a flower, or a person, or the moon one at a time, like a series of photographic slides, not only will we be bored but we will feel anxious as well, seeing only a world of sepa-rateness. We cannot truly appreciate life if we just see things individu-ally because that is not their fundamental nature.

A garden exists because flowers, bushes, grasses, and trees have relationships with each other. The flower has the form of a flower, and at the same time the flower is empty. Inherently, it is formless. If the flower insisted on maintaining "itself," the garden could not exist. In the same way, a nation, a community, or a family exists because peo-ple have relationships. When we are able to give up our small selves, we have good relationships. But if we insist on being strictly "our-selves," that is, if we cling to ideas of who we are, we create bound-aries and separate ourselves from others. We cannot, however, insist on being separate because inherently we are always in relationship. Our empty nature requires us continuously to be part of relation-ships.

Communities, families, nations, and gardens can truly exist when there is no stubbornness. To practice with others and join with the community is the Buddhist way. At the same time, we have to make our own personal efforts and express ourselves in our daily lives. The background of our daily practice is strong faith in our inherent rela-tionships with all things. When we have that trust, anything we do is the expression of our fundamental nature.

Zazen practice is based on our inherent emptiness. Because noth-ing is permanent, there is nothing to grasp. Without this understand-ing, our practice is limited, aimed at achieving a personal goal. Even when we feel that we have attained our goal, if our feeling is not based on true understanding, practice cannot help us. Our effort has to be based on our fundamental nature, our empty minds that are always ready to be in relationship with someone or something. To appreciate the true quality of our practice in relationship with people and things is the meaning behind our effort.

A random collection of individual plants cannot create a garden, even though each one may be very beautiful. They must have some relationship with each other to create a balanced, peaceful garden.

a case of politics: a story

On a balmy summer day in 1973, my manager, Ray, strolled into my office, slowly and silently closed the door, carefully sat down, and, with uncharacteristic precision, put his feet up on my desk. He always seemed to have his feet up, even when working alone in his office. It was a sign of his relaxed manner. He was a hard-working individual of few words, in his late fifties, having been with IBM over twenty-five years. His management style was pragmatic and easygoing. Not interested in power or personal ambition, he was easy to get along with and had a dry sense of humor, although I sometimes had to coax it out of him. I liked Ray, both as a person and as a manager.

Rather than look me in the eye, he absently fiddled with some papers on my desk while he told me that I had to lower the performance appraisal rating for Paul, one of the young men in my department. He went on to explain, a little too casually I thought, that the new president of our division had reviewed employee performance statistics and concluded that the numerical appraisal ratings were artificially high. In an executive letter to the upper management of the division, the president outlined his belief that managers were not encouraging their employees to meet high standards of productivity and quality but instead were being too lenient in evaluating work performance.

I was stunned. I didn't understand how statistical data could lead an executive to conclude that several hundred competent managers were failing to provide the leadership expected of them. At best, the numbers indicated that appraisal ratings might be artificially high. But the president's first impression of such a critical feature of IBM's management capabilities had to be verified by more careful investigation. The new president had a reputation for being a strong decision maker, but I thought that his executive letter was premature.

In addition, even if it were true that ratings were too high over-all, it would be an injustice to downgrade Paul's—or anybody's—performance rating retroactively for something he did not do. Not only would it be unfair to Paul but it would be a poor business decision as well. Paul would be upset and most likely tell others what happened; the morale of the department would be damaged, in turn affecting productivity, creativity, and quality. I asked Ray, "Why are you singling out Paul? It's already been a month since I gave him that performance rating, and you approved of it at the time."

He responded, "He isn't being singled out. A month isn't too long to change the rating."

I said, "What if it were three months?"

He replied, "That would be different."

As far as I was concerned, one month or three months made no difference: retroactive downgrading was unfair if the original performance assessment had been judged to be accurate. Now I was confused by our conversation. IBM had a philosophy, as well as a reputation, of treating employees fairly. Managers were trained to be impartial and honest. I appreciated this humane quality; it made the very large corporation a secure place to work, a place where management could be trusted. This was one of the major reasons that I liked working there. So I was disappointed by what my boss was telling me and what he was asking me to do. I argued again that it would be a mistake.

Despite my reasoning, Ray insisted that I downgrade Paul's rating. I continued to insist that doing so would cause harm to Paul as well as to the work environment. Although we argued, it was not a heated exchange; we tried to reason with each other. But Ray and I were at a stalemate, so we went to see his boss.

John was also in his late fifties and had been with IBM for many years. He, too, was down-to-earth and easygoing. But he was different from Ray in one aspect: he was personally ambitious and politically very savvy. That did not prevent me from liking him.

In fact, I had recommended him for his present job—as my boss's boss—during a reorganization two years earlier.

John was more insistent than Ray had been. Impatiently, he dismissed my argument about retroactive downgrading, saying that we had to do something *now*. I asked who it was that wanted appraisal ratings downgraded in order to change the statistics: the new president or John's own management? He said, "What's the difference? The managers have to stick together."

I explained that John was asking me to do something that was unfair to Paul and that could destroy the trust I had developed with the people in my department. I pointed out the irony: if I went against my own conscience and judgment to do what was being asked, IBM would hold *me* responsible for the loss of morale and subsequent loss of productivity.

But John was not willing to be flexible. Instead, he made it sound like what he was asking me to do was absolutely necessary. It was clear to me that he did not want to displease his own management. He finally said, "If you can't do it, we'll get somebody who can."

We weren't getting any closer. With each exchange, we became slightly more polarized. Yet until this moment, our argument had been impersonal, a reasonable difference of opinion within the boundaries of acceptable IBM give-and-take. Now John's threat signaled that the discussion was over, leaving me with a difficult choice: compromise my principles or lose my job.

Normally, John was not an unreasonable man. In this case, however, I felt that he could not see the injustice of what he was asking. Or, if he did see it, he did not care to take a stand with his own manager. Either way, I felt betrayed by the system, which stressed fairness and honesty in employee relations. I took a stand. Emotion rushed to my face as I stiffened and said that I couldn't do what he was asking because it was unethical and unwise. I left John's office certain that I would soon have another job. A week later, there was a reorganization, and I was given a new assignment. A few days after that, Paul's new manager downgraded his appraisal.

I was aware that business politics often forces hard choices and influences careers, but I was upset that in this case personal politics took precedence over fairness and good judgment. I considered leaving IBM but knew that it would be a futile gesture. As a protest, it would change nothing. In addition, personal politics exists everywhere. Where could I go to escape it?

Despite incidents of this kind, brought about by personal ambition and desire for power, IBM was inherently an ethical organization. It would have been a mistake for me to condemn the entire company for this one episode. I decided that I had done what I believed to be right in a catch-22 situation.

Several weeks after the incident, though, I realized that I had made a mistake. When threatened with the "or else" ultimatum, I had insisted on being right and taken a position that left no room to continue discussion. A better, more flexible response might have been to say, "Are you sure we have no alternative?" followed with, "Then help me find the best way to do this." We might not have found a better way, but by becoming stubborn I had thrown away the opportunity to try.

I had lost sight of why I was arguing with my management in the first place. Concern for unfairness to Paul had turned into a defense of my own values. I lost focus, concerned less about preventing needless suffering than about adhering to an abstract principle. At some point, I should have realized that I was not going to win the argument, that there would be no compromise. Given the inevitability of Paul's rating being downgraded, it would have been better for me to have agreed to do the distasteful task myself, rather than leave it up to his new manager. Paul and I were pretty close. I could have explained to him that the incident would not affect his career in the long run, and, because he trusted me, I might have been able to take some of the sting out of the disappointment. More important, I would have remained his manager, in the best position to make it up to Paul as soon as feasible. But I had let my emotions and my ego get in the way, so we both lost.

In this case, I failed to see that I did not have to rush into an either-or trade-off, that idealism does not have to clash with reality in everyday affairs. Both compassion—our response to suffering—and pragmatism—doing what is necessary in a given situation—can be expressed in the complex circumstances of daily life by understanding the aspirations and concerns of people we work with and by envisioning the long-range unfolding, the ever-widening ripples, of our present actions. Our awareness is the prelude to establishing creative, helpful relationships, setting the stage for speaking and acting with skillful means. We can develop such relationships not by applying clever techniques or analyzing personalities but simply by setting aside emotions and paying attention to what is happening in each situation. However, in the pressure of everyday life, a mind can become closed and blinded by its own fears and desires. That's what I let happen to me.

Paul left IBM within six months for a new career in real estate. He soon became a developer and was doing very well the last time I spoke with him. His leaving was IBM's loss, and mine as well.

CHAPTER 8

the adventure
continues

By 1977, Haiku Zendo could no longer accommodate the number of people who wanted to attend on Wednesday evenings, the night of Kobun's weekly lecture. Parking was also a problem. So the group decided it was time to move to larger quarters, to establish a public facility that would provide more space.

We embarked on a fund-raising effort, and in two years we had enough money to purchase two properties. The first included several acres that had recently been an alternative high school in the Santa Cruz mountains above Los Gatos. This became the "country center," which we named Jikoji. In addition, we found a small church for sale not far from downtown Mountain View. It became our "city center." We named it Kannon Do, or "Place of Compassion."

We started using Kannon Do in the fall of 1979, following a summer of converting the Pentecostal church to a meditation hall. Several residents were still living on the country property, so Jikoji needed almost two years to become useful as a retreat center. Kobun was the teacher at both places. Because of its location in the heart of the heavily populated Santa Clara Valley, accessible by both bus and train and within a fifteen-minute drive of most of its current participants, my interest was in Kannon Do. Many felt the same way, while other former Haiku Zendo members preferred Jikoji's rural atmosphere.

At Kannon Do, we continued early-morning meditation as well as the Wednesday evening and Saturday morning schedules.

Meditation retreats were held at both centers. Kobun would attend Jikoji retreats, while I acted as a focal point at Kannon Do. Kobun continued to lecture Wednesday evenings at Kannon Do. Over time, though, he asked me to give more of these weekly talks.

At the conclusion of separate, concurrent meditation retreats in April of 1983, the two groups joined at Jikoji for an informal closing ceremony. When we were gathered together in the meditation hall, Kobun asked me to join him in the center of the room. He then announced, "Starting now, Les is the teacher at Kannon Do," and he presented me with a teaching staff traditionally carried by Zen teachers. I was so startled I couldn't move. After a few moments, he grabbed my arm and pushed the stick into my hand. The announcement shocked all of us. He had given no indication that he had anything like this in mind.

From then on, Kobun rarely came to Kannon Do. I was on my own to figure out how to carry on the spiritual practice of the Zen teachers who had come from Japan, to provide an environment that would encourage practice. Many of the people who considered Kobun their spiritual teacher also stopped coming to Kannon Do. For about a year, it was up to a half dozen of us to continue the practice and make it available for newcomers. Mondays through Fridays, I was usually by myself at the 5:30 A.M. zazen period. Our initial meditation retreats were attended by two or three people. But little by little, an increasing number discovered Kannon Do.

In late 1983, Kobun told me that it was time for my Dharma transmission. This ceremony acknowledges the teaching capacity and autonomy of a Zen monk. It is a private, face-to-face ceremony, much like an initiation, symbolizing both the emergence of the monk as a new teacher and the continuation of the lineage.

In the Zen tradition, acknowledgment of a monk's readiness to be independent can only be granted by his or her teacher. So I was surprised when Kobun told me that my Dharma transmission should be performed in Japan by Suzuki-roshi's son and successor, Hoitsu Suzuki-roshi. I told Kobun that I felt that he had been my formal teacher following the death of Suzuki-roshi, since he and I had practiced together for so many years. But he said that it is best not to change lineages, and that his lineage was not the same as Suzuki-roshi's. He explained further that he had promised Suzuki-roshi that he would take care of me until I was ready.

It was then that I understood that Kobun had never intended for me to have a formal teacher-student relationship with him because he did not want to take Suzuki-roshi's place. So for nearly thirteen years, he had purposely kept some distance between us, avoiding me so that I would not rely on him as a teacher but would work things out for myself. He had forced me to make my own discoveries.

I reminded Kobun that I was a virtual stranger to Hoitsu Suzuki, having met him just briefly during his father's illness. Would Hoitsu agree to perform this important ceremony, which is traditionally based on years of intimate practice together? Kobun agreed to call Hoitsu in Japan and explain the situation. A week later, he told me that everything was arranged and to contact Hoitsu myself to establish dates for a visit. Hoitsu invited Mary and me to stay for two weeks at his family temple, Rinsoin, in the fishing town of Yaizu, near Shizuoka, midway between Tokyo and Kyoto on Japan's east coast.

Mary and I went to Japan for a month in the early spring of 1984. In addition to our stay with Hoitsu and his family, our trip included visits to friends on the northern island of Hokkaido, to Kobun's family temple, and one week as tourists in Kyoto. When we arrived at Rinsoin, we discovered that the temple was being prepared for a major event to occur the following week. Five hundred laypeople were to receive Buddhist precepts in a ceremony that would last several days. It had been over thirty-five years since this ceremony had taken place at Rinsoin. Carpenters and electricians, including several of Hoitsu's friends from high school days, were everywhere, repairing six-hundred-year-old Rinsoin and preparing it for the ceremony. Hoitsu's gracious and hardworking wife, Chitose, was busy managing the repair and decoration inside the temple and taking care of her three children, as well as ensuring that all of us were fed and housed.

Clearly, there was to be no Dharma transmission ceremony. Hoitsu did not mention the subject. I wondered what Kobun had told him. So on our first evening at Rinsoin, when Mary, Chitose, Hoitsu, and I were becoming acquainted over traditional late-night tea and sake, I told the Suzukis that Kobun had sent me for Dharma transmission.

The temple was silent except for the *Chu-chun, chu-chun* call of the white wagtail in the forest surrounding Rinsoin. Hoitsu and his wife looked at me and at each other with surprise. Hoitsu said, "Isn't Chino-sensei taking care of that for you?" I explained my relationship to Kobun after Hoitsu's father had died. They were very puzzled. They thought we had come to Japan to help them prepare for Rinsoin's Buddhist precepts ceremony.

Years earlier, the ambiguity would have troubled me. But now, as we walked to our room along the dark corridor, lit only by occasional intrusions of moonlight that found their way through the guardian gate of the temple, I was unconcerned by the miscommunication. I did not feel compelled to immediately straighten out the misunderstanding, as I would have in a similar situation at work. I was even surprised to feel a lightheartedness about the whole thing. This sense of confident indifference came from the recognition that my mind was becoming increasingly flexible, less and less bothered by uncertainty. Both my "careers" had showed me the corrosive effects of clinging to expectations. I was learning to let them go and be ready for anything. I decided not to speak of the subject again. The important thing was to enjoy the remainder of our vacation and not get caught up in what might or might not happen in the future.

The next day, Chitose put us to work. We joined an endless stream of family friends and temple members from Yaizu who came to help with chores and provide meals for the workers. The tasks were endless. Rinsoin had once housed several Zen monks who maintained the large temple as part of their training. But for over fifty years, it had not been used as a training temple. The Suzuki family were its only permanent residents and caretakers. Many areas of the temple and grounds needed repair and cleaning. Among other things, Mary and I learned how to remove and replace rice paper from sliding windows and shoji screens. I undertook a major effort to clean several generations of algae and repair the water circulation system of a huge fishpond. This dramatic, two-day event created great interest among our new Yaizu friends.

In the evenings, everyone stayed for dinner, and the work continued until 9:00 P.M. or so, followed by a celebration of tea, sake, and more food. We all took delight in the hard work and preparation for the important ceremony. It was a joyous community. We developed warm relationships with the Suzukis' friends and temple members. Late each night, Mary and I deepened our new friendship with Hoitsu and Chitose. After the women had gone to bed, Hoitsu and I frequently stayed up until 2:00 A.M., smoking our pipes and talking, listening to the wind and rain in the tea plants growing on the side of Yaizu mountain.

At 6:00 A.M. each day, Hoitsu and I sat together in zazen in the ancient Rinsoin zendo. It was a strange feeling. I thought about the monks who had sat here over the centuries, continuing and preserving the traditional practice. Now here I was, trying to absorb the spirit of the place so that I could help bring it to America.

Three days before the precepts ceremony was to take place, a dozen or so senior Zen priests arrived from various temples in Japan to help with the final preparations. Mary and I had to relinquish our living quarters, overlooking the rock garden and rejuvenated fishpond, to a high-ranking roshi who was to dedicate the ceremony. We were reestablished in Hoitsu's pottery shed.

When Mary developed a cold, we decided that it was time to trade the crowd, the chaos, the chilliness, and the damp of Rinsoin for the warmth and quiet of an inn at Kyoto. We remained at Rinsoin for two days of the ceremony. Hoitsu wanted us to stay longer, but Mary was not well. On our last night, Hoitsu said to me, "Come back next year at the same time for Dharma transmission. It will take one month. Leave your wife at home."

The following April, I returned to Rinsoin. Each day began with zazen, followed by breakfast and a visit with the Suzuki family. Most of my days were spent preparing for the ceremony and taking care of Rinsoin. I chopped firewood and tended the fifty-year-old boiler that provided the temple's hot water. I washed dishes, hung laundry, cleaned toilets, swept and dusted the temple, replaced flowers, cleaned incense burners and ashtrays, and weeded the temple grounds. It was a monk's life.

Late one afternoon, as the warmth of early spring lingered on the earth and the sun began its descent behind the deep green tea forest, I worked my way on hands and knees along the bank of the creek that flowed down the mountain behind Rinsoin's kitchen, pulling out overgrown grasses. Suddenly, a large, brown, speckled lizard ran out from a bush, stopping within a few inches of my face. Unafraid, he stared at me, right in the eye. Unmoving, both of us on all fours, we were nose to nose for an eternity, perhaps a full five seconds. As he scampered away, as quickly as he had appeared, I was left with an expansive feeling of warmth, comfort, and peace.

The sanction of Dharma transmission in May of 1985 did not signal that I had achieved anything special or advanced to some kind of higher stage of spiritual practice. The ceremony simply expressed Hoitsu's trust in my determination to continue the practice of his teacher—his father—and to make it available to others. It also meant that I accepted responsibility for carrying the practice and passing it on to the next generation.

journey of discovery

Our spiritual path must be a journey without a map. This journey is not the same for any two of us, yet it is the same for everyone. If our spiritual way were predictable, if it had precise starting and ending points, we would all follow a carefully designed plan. But if that were so, we would have no chance of understanding our lives—the exploration and discovery would already be completed. The only way to appreciate our lives and their meaning is to make our own spiritual discoveries.

With the help of the Internet, a travel agent, or the local automobile club, we can get directions to go from one place to another. But a true spiritual path is not a road or highway that someone else can map out for us. It has no overnight stops, no resting places, no motels. We can never say, "We are partway there." Yet because it has no starting point and no destination, we can travel in Buddha's world, the world of enlightenment.

Each of us has our own unique life, made up of our everyday activities. At the same time, all of our lives are ready to be Buddha's life when we really want to express our true selves. We do this when we allow each everyday activity to express who we really are. Thus we can express our true nature *because* we live ordinary lives, not in spite of them. There is no need to wait to express ourselves. We are not training to express ourselves in the future. Our true nature needs to be expressed now, in this moment and in every moment.

Because we are human, it is not easy for us to perform an activity without expecting to get something in return for our effort. In addition, very often we cannot take the time to work as completely and carefully as we would like because of our society's emphasis on meeting short-term objectives. Faced with these difficulties, each of us has to find his or her own way to put practice into daily life. Every one of us has to create our own map; it is easy to become lost. Zazen practice enables us to know where we are.

When the basis of our daily effort is practice, we start each activity with the understanding that we are expressing something other than our personal intention. Inherently we know that our activity is expressing something universal. So we try to continue our activity without distraction but with quiet, ready minds. If we become aware that we are distracted, we simply return to our empty minds so that we can take care of our activity completely.

We can express our true nature when we give up self-oriented ideas and totally involve ourselves in our activity. This is true even if we are not consciously aware of our true nature. If we insist on trying to attain a discrete, identifiable experience of our true nature expressing itself, then our true nature cannot be expressed. The desires of our conscious minds prevent our true selves from being expressed in our activities. We lose our way if we try to follow a discrete spiritual path because none exists. It is enough for us to continue our quiet, aware minds and to have a feeling of expressing something very great. With our own everyday lives, each of us goes ahead on this spiritual journey of discovery. Going ahead with ready minds, we always know where we are.

enlightenment at work

the vehicle: a story

I greeted my boss as I walked through the open door of his office. "Hey, Barry, got a minute?"

He looked up from the accounting reports he was working on, put down his pencil, leaned back with his arms stretched behind his head, and said, "Sure, come on in."

"I need to talk to you about something."

"It's Alex, isn't it?"

"That's right, it is."

My manager was a perceptive, no-nonsense kind of person. He was self-reliant, hardworking, and disciplined. At the same time, he was fair and easygoing. He had a big laugh and a big, booming voice. His uncanny knack for knowing what was going on was gained by staying tuned in: getting out of his office, dropping in on people, asking how they were doing, having a friendly chat, exchanging personal stories. People recognized that he was genuinely interested in them. They trusted him, and they respected his judgment.

Two years earlier, I had hired Alex as a systems analyst. It was his first job out of college. He got off to a good start, and in the beginning, everything went well. But in the past six months it had become clear that he was having a hard time. Barry and I had talked about it when we'd reviewed Alex's last appraisal rating, which was below average.

"How's he doing?" Barry asked, although he knew.

"Not so good," I replied. "He has trouble planning his activities. He doesn't seem to be able to figure out what to do first, and what relies on what. He also has a hard time grasping the scope of a problem. He doesn't ask meaningful questions."

"In what way?"

"Well, for example, last week I suggested that he go talk to Sally McGuire, the manager over in production control, to understand the changes they plan to make in their system."

"Sally's easy to get along with. She knows what she's doing. How did it go?"

"When he came back, he said that he'd had a good meeting with her. But when I asked him about their new procedures compared with how they do things today, he was at a loss."

Alex was a very likable young man. He was well educated, enthusiastic, and hardworking. But as he gained experience and was given increasing freedom to manage his own work, he wasn't able to respond. He still needed to be told what to do as well as how to do it. He didn't seem to have any ideas of his own.

"What else?" Barry asked. "How does he communicate?"

"Not well. He still has trouble explaining himself, and his writing isn't too clear."

We talked more about Alex and the kinds of difficulties he was having. We felt badly. But something had to be done.

From its inception early in this century until a few years ago, IBM had maintained an unofficial "no layoff" policy. It gave no hard guarantees of continued employment, yet in practice the company provided work, without reduction in salary or professional level, to any employee whose job was eliminated or whose work assignment ended. No one was laid off for economic or business reasons. This policy also meant that no employee could be fired for doing a poor job without first being granted sufficient opportunity and time to improve his or her performance.

Providing an environment of stability and fairness, this long-range view encouraged trust, loyalty, and dedication to company goals. It helped create the famous IBM culture, which in the eyes of some skeptics diminished motivation but which was actually extremely effective in maintaining high morale, teamwork, and a disciplined work ethic, all contributing to IBM's long history of success. To make this policy effective, managers were required to share responsibility for maintaining the quality of their employees' performance, to work with them as much as necessary in removing obstacles to getting the job done.

When we were finished, Barry summarized what the company expected of me as Alex's manager. "OK, here's what you have to do," he began. "Make sure that he knows his situation, that he's not meeting the requirements of the job. Be very specific about those requirements. Give him examples. Make sure he understands what he needs to be doing and in what ways he isn't providing it.

"Start meeting with him on a weekly basis," Barry continued. "Make sure he understands that you are doing this to help him improve his skills and performance. Work with him to develop weekly objectives and plans that you and he agree on. If he has trouble meeting the goals, point out exactly how and explain specifically what he can do to improve. Say things constructively, without criticizing. Tell him that he will have another appraisal rating in three months and that if he can't meet the requirements of the job after six months, he will have to be let go."

We spent another half hour or so discussing ways for me to coach Alex in hopes of turning around his situation.

Alex and I started to have our weekly meetings. He acknowledged his situation. He was concerned but seemed encouraged that we would be working together. We had no problem developing specific weekly goals and plans. But as we reviewed his progress over the next several weeks, it was clear that he was still having trouble. Sometimes he would forget to take care of a work item on his plan. Sometimes he would do it only partially. When

I pointed out a discrepancy, he would agree enthusiastically, as if I were giving him some vital piece of information that he could use. But similar problems would recur.

This went on for two months, until Alex came to my office unexpectedly. "Do you have a minute?" he asked.

"Sure, come in. How's it going?"

"Look," he said, "I know what's happening. Things aren't working out, and I can see the handwriting on the wall. So here's my letter of resignation. I got another job over in Fremont. I'd like to leave in two weeks, if that's OK with you."

I had mixed feelings. I was sorry that Alex's career with IBM hadn't worked out, especially since I had hired him. At the same time, I was glad that he had taken it upon himself to make a change, that he wasn't going to be hurt. I was especially pleased by what he said next.

"You know, I want to thank you for the way you handled this. I really learned a lot working here."

Alex left IBM two weeks later, following the customary farewell party of coffee and cake. Only he, Barry, and I knew that there had been some difficulty. Everyone congratulated him on his new career opportunity.

This story is an example of how even a large institution can have a heart when it places a high priority on relationships with people. IBM's approach to problems such as Alex's was both compassionate and disciplined. I could have acted as a passive vehicle for conveying company policy. But the values reflected by this policy are embedded in spiritual practice—mindfulness, patience, attentive listening, seeing the big picture, caring for the individual—so I willingly gave serious attention to being an active vehicle for these values.

In daily life, each of us is a vehicle for something. Our choices of values determine the kinds of vehicles we are, the way we move in the world and relate to each other. All individuals and all organizations are free to choose values that they feel are important, that express their vision. Seeing ourselves as vehicles for something greater than ourselves, we naturally choose spiritual values.

Like Holden of *The Catcher in the Rye*, many of us are often confused about expressing our inherent compassion, our concern for the difficulties of others. So we look for heroes and admire their unselfish courage. But, in reality, we ourselves are heroes when we continue spiritual practice in all of life's activities. Emphasizing mindfulness and selflessness in relationships, we have no need to search for heroes outside ourselves. There is nothing "sacred" beyond our present effort.

friendliness

In Buddhism and in Zen practice, compassion is accompanied by a light, confident, and stable feeling about life. And because it is based on understanding the true nature of our lives, joy is also part of compassion. Naturally, when we meet or hear about people who are suffering, we feel sympathy for them. But Buddhist compassion is much wider and deeper than a particular feeling for one individual or group. Buddhist compassion is to see each life situation as it really is, in its totality.

Universal compassion begins with compassion for ourselves. But it doesn't mean self-pity. Instead, it means that we have a sense for what is taking place in us and through us. When we have this awareness of what is really happening, we appreciate that we are the vehicles for these things to happen and we want to take care of these vehicles and preserve them. We also want to help others have the same awareness. Our desire to take care of what we recognize about ourselves is the start of Buddhist compassion.

We become aware of what is truly taking place in us and in our lives through practice. In zazen, we become friendly to ourselves. Compassion starts with this very intimate friendship, which extends to people we already know and to new people we meet. It even extends to people we haven't met. This feeling of friendliness that reaches out to people everywhere is an expression of our sense of oneness.

But we cannot be friendly to others if we are not friendly to ourselves. Many of us do not allow ourselves to feel what is happening in us and through us, do not permit ourselves to be aware of what we are really doing and to appreciate what is really happening. This is because we do not have confidence in who we really are. Without this confidence, we cannot be friendly to ourselves or to others. Without this trust in what we are doing, we cannot understand our lives.

Buddha pointed out that human suffering is based on our desire for material and emotional things, transient and impermanent things, which can never fully satisfy us. Yet, even though we may strive for these things because we think they will bring us happiness, they are not the objectives of our true desire. What we really want is something that will fill up an empty inner space. Our desire for things that are impermanent is an expression of our true desire to feel complete. If we do not attain material and emotional things, we become disappointed and suffer. If we do attain them, we fall into the trap of self-satisfaction. Even though our egos may be temporarily satisfied, we cannot be truly satisfied because we cannot hold on to these transient, unreal things. But our rational minds are unaware of the trap, so we continue to strive to attain things that cannot last.

In Zen practice, we turn our efforts away from trying to attain something for ourselves. We turn our attention to friendliness, which is independent of attainment. We usually select our personal friends carefully and exclusively, after we have developed some relationship with them. But Buddhist friendliness is not exclusive; it includes everyone. It is impossible to be truly friendly to ourselves and at the same time limit the friendship we extend to others.

We may think, "I do zazen to take care of my own practice and my own life; my practice does not include other people." But it is impossible to exclude others from true spiritual practice. When friendliness flows from zazen, we do not need to make a special effort to share it. We naturally feel generous toward everyone. This is the meaning of compassion.

If we do not understand that we are already inherently complete, we continue to strive for emotional or material things. We have a poor attitude, not in the sense of "bad" but in the sense of "needy." However, in truth we are already wealthy. We do not need to strive for anything, and there is no reason not to be generous.

Even if we have nothing material to share, we can share ourselves. We lose nothing when we give ourselves away. When we feel this truth, we become friendly and generous. But it is necessary to trust our inherent completeness. If we do not have this trust, we will always feel poor in the midst of great wealth.

Buddhist compassion does not mean being a saint or a hero. It starts with the simple feeling of friendship that flows from zazen practice. Buddha's practice is naturally generous. When we have a warm and confident feeling about life, we see that compassion is everywhere and everything is taking care of everything.

expressing encouragement

Each of us is inherently complete, only we do not realize it. Because of our delusions and our attachments to the appearances of the material world, we fool ourselves into believing that we are incomplete. But instead of trying to grow or be transformed into someone else, we should emphasize expressing without limitation who we are, who we have always been.

On the other hand, in the dynamic activities of daily life, it is possible to expand our understanding and change the kinds of things we say and do and the ways we do them. But here, too, it is a mistake to try to change other people, because the responsibility for changing how we think and behave belongs to each of us individually. So instead of trying to have people accept our way of doing something or our way of understanding, our emphasis should be on finding ways to encourage them to expand their own understanding. If we attempt to change others' minds simply by trying to sell them our ideas, we are actually seeking something for ourselves. Encouraging other people to expand their own understanding without pushing our understanding on them is one of the greatest gifts we can give.

We shouldn't ignore people who are having difficulty. At the same time, we have to be careful not to interfere with their practice; to do so will only discourage them. We have to find a middle way, which includes encouraging each other with our own practice and acting or speaking helpfully according to the circumstances.

Zen Master Dogen taught that practice and enlightenment are not separate. In his writing, he encouraged people to emphasize practice and not be caught by ideas about enlightenment. So in this practice, we don't worry about trying to change ourselves or others. Enlightenment always exists, it is everywhere, there is no end to it. We just naturally express our true nature in our lives, moment after moment.

True self appears when we actively practice in the present moment, not waiting for inherent enlightenment to appear in some special way. We do not think about it, and we do not worry about it. We just appreciate that it exists continuously and that we must continuously express it. So our practice is dedicated to something that cannot be described. We always express the inexpressible in our activity. There is no need to change anything.

True nature is continuously moving and creating. This is our fundamental nature, who we are. We should emphasize this dynamic nature of enlightenment by actively practicing with our lives. This doesn't mean just keeping busy. It means that we should know what we are doing. If we become attached to some intellectual idea of our lives, our lives will be in vain. They will be tied up in knots, and we will not be free. The way of zazen practice is to drop off the ropes of discrimination.

equanimity: a story

On my first visit to Eiheiji monastery, I struck up a conversation with one of the young resident monks who spoke English well. He was intrigued by the growing interest in Zen in America. We had been talking for about ten minutes when a short, heavyset monk began screaming in Japanese at my new friend. The language did not prevent me from recognizing that he was being reprimanded for doing something other than his assigned task. The rebuke lasted about a minute; it seemed unnecessarily severe. When the short monk turned and stormed away, the young monk smiled and quietly said, "I must go now. Nice to meet you."

I was startled by the harshness and what appeared to be lack of care that I had witnessed. I wondered if the display was intentional or simply reflected the personality of the shorter monk. It seemed more appropriate to a military boot camp than to a monastery. I was also struck by the poise and patience of the younger monk in the face of severe criticism. Is this part of a Zen monk's training? I wondered. Is this the way wisdom and compassion are encouraged? The episode was a striking illustration of how our attitude to personal criticism is a defining factor in our spiritual outlook and in an enlightened response to a sometimes unfriendly world.

Suzuki-roshi once spoke about the need to find out for ourselves how to do something without instinctively relying on rules or asking for help, including what we learn from making mistakes and accepting criticism. He described an incident in his own training as a young monk:

When I was at Eiheiji Monastery in Japan serving my teacher, helping my teacher, he did not tell us anything, but whenever we made a mistake, he scolded. It is a kind of rule to open a sliding door from the right side. This is the usual way. There is a little round hole to open the screen. One day as I was starting to open it, I was scolded: "Don't open it that way! Not that side!" So the next morning I opened it from the other side and got scolded again. I didn't know what to do. But I found out that the day I opened the right side, my teacher's guest had been on the right side. To open the right-hand side is the rule, but because that morning his guest was there, I should have opened it from the other side. Before I open the door I should find out which side the guest is on.[1]

Without explanation, Suzuki-roshi's master scolded him, not because he was irresponsible but because he wanted him to pay attention, to discover things for himself. By accepting the criticism without emotion, with equanimity, the young Suzuki resolved his question, thereby deepening his capacity to see the big picture.

communication

Business is supposed to be a rational activity, based as it is on carefully reasoned ideas and principles, supported by unemotional research, opinion surveys, testing of new products, and the scrutiny of venture capitalists. You would think that the business of science, technology, and engineering, the most rational of disciplines, would be even more free from irrational behavior. But this assumption is not rational, since we know that business is an activity of human beings, emotionally volatile creatures.

Business reflects human nature, both its rational side and its emotional side. It is the emotional at work that can get us into trouble, creating angry feelings, stress, and torn relationships. Instead of a supportive, cooperative climate of good sense and community, we often create an atmosphere of individuals at odds with each other. This is not universally true; many companies are well-known for their congenial work environments. But when self-orientation and ambition are overemphasized, there is the danger of personal competition hurting individuals and the organization.

meeting with mindfulness: a story

An unanticipated problem had erupted. During the development of a companywide procedure that was intended to save money and improve the accuracy and timeliness of certain administrative information, one of the organizations that depended on the data suddenly decided not to use the new system but to continue using its old procedures instead. The success of the new system depended on the participation of all affected organizations, so this group's holdout threatened a project that had already taken several months. A meeting was called to resolve the crisis.

> FIRST MANAGER: I don't understand why you say it's no good.
> SECOND MANAGER (from the "holdout" organization): I told you, it doesn't buy us anything.
> THIRD MANAGER: Look, you agreed to use—
> FOURTH MANAGER: And these guys changed specifications just for you. I thought that cleared up your—
> SECOND MANAGER: No, we never agreed—
> FIRST MANAGER: Oh, come on! Back in July, you said—
> SECOND MANAGER: Hey, we never committed—
> FIRST MANAGER: Damn it, let me finish!
> FOURTH MANAGER: Your boss signed the agreement letter.
> FIFTH MANAGER: What's your problem, anyhow?
> SECOND MANAGER: What do you mean, my problem? I told you at the start we were happy with our current system.
> THIRD MANAGER: We went through all that political crap last year. Now you're—
> SECOND MANAGER: Don't tell me how to run my business. This whole thing is a joke.

We got out late, very late. As we walked back to our offices, my boss said, "You were pretty quiet in there."

"I didn't have anything to add," I said.

He replied, "Yes, you did. You should have spoken up."

And I said, "Well, you know, it was crazy in there, with all that interrupting and finger-pointing. Half the time I didn't know what was going on. What I had to say wouldn't have made any difference."

"Yeah, but you should have spoken up anyhow."

What had happened that afternoon was not so unusual. Too often, meetings were not very effective. Was everyone in collusion about bad meetings? It seemed like standard practice, an agreed-to part of working life: meetings are fundamentally awful and nothing can be done about it.

The mission of the product development laboratory was to create new IBM products. An engineering project was successful if it could build a model of a new product—a prototype—that provided the needed functions and reliability while meeting financial objectives. Simply, the goal of the development engineers was to produce one thing, the first of a new product line. From this prototype, the manufacturing organization would produce hundreds, even thousands, to fulfill customer orders.

My concern about the ineffectiveness of meetings started me thinking about what was fundamentally taking place in the product development laboratory. In manufacturing, the process could be scientifically evaluated by collecting test data from a large statistical sample of new machines as they came through production. But how could the process in the engineering laboratory be measured if we only produced *one*? What was our real "product" and what was our "process"?

I decided that the actual product of the approximately two-year product development period was the *knowledge* that comes from creativity and problem solving. These days it is known in legal terms as intellectual property. It was in meetings that this knowledge was shared and problems were resolved. I decided that meetings, both technical and administrative, were at the heart of our process. It was vitally important for us to have effective meetings. When meetings are chaotic, people tune out, just like I had done.

I was not surprised to learn, through an informal survey, that a majority of managers and engineers felt that more than half the meetings they attended were less than 50 percent effective. We were squandering not just money but enthusiasm and morale as well.

I started to pay more attention to the dynamics of meetings so that I could understand how they went wrong. In the first place, I recognized problems related to the mechanics: poor agenda, unclear objectives, absence of commitments, lack of action plans. But these essentially administrative oversights could be corrected with better planning and organization. More important, and more difficult to resolve, were the interpersonal difficulties: attempts to dominate, tuning out, digressions, interruptions, and disruptions. These problems were created by emotions related to the need for personal recognition and control. Meetings often became competitive battlegrounds.

The need for frequent meetings meant that many people were making life miserable for themselves and for each other. Their frustrations at meetings spilled over into other areas of work. If meetings, and the entire workplace, were to be satisfying, feelings and personal needs, as well as creative ideas, had to be considered. After studying the art and methods of running meetings, including attending professional classes and workshops, I eventually developed a class that emphasized the use of facilitation techniques.

When I first learned these skills, I was impressed by their similarity to the personal qualities emphasized in Buddhism and Zen practice. For example, the first thing a facilitator must do is *set aside personal feelings* about what is going on—forget the desires that make up a "private agenda" in order not to filter or distort what is being said. He or she has to listen and respond without bias. Otherwise, the group will not trust the facilitator and the meeting will not succeed.

The second thing a facilitator must do is *maintain awareness of the total situation*, of all the emotions and energies in the room, especially how they are changing. To have this big picture, the facilitator must practice Big Mind, that is, keep his or her mind ready to accept whatever is happening without mentally criticizing or judging anything expressed by anyone in the meeting.

Third, the facilitator must *encourage creative relationships* by emphasizing the positive. For example, when a suggestion is made, the facilitator ensures that its evaluation starts positively, that is, with what the critic *likes* about the idea. Only then can the critic move on to talk about elements of the suggestion that might be improved. With this approach, the facilitator creates a supportive environment, where no one feels threatened by criticism.

Helping the group reach consensus is another high-priority quality of a facilitator. With consensus, there are no losers. Everyone feels included in the decision; there is no feeling of separation. Consensus helps to establish a creative sense of purpose among the participants.

The fifth and perhaps most powerful facilitator technique, I discovered, is to *acknowledge the ideas and feelings of everyone in the room*. This recognition enabled me to realize that the source of most anger—both personal and collective—is lack of acknowledgment from other people. And it was true, I realized, not just in meetings but in all aspects of daily life. Patient, attentive listening with positive, encouraging feedback—both verbally and with gestures—are necessary to promote creativity and goodwill and to prevent destructive emotions.

Facilitator techniques turned out to be, for me, equivalent to the skillful means of Buddhism. They create a collaborative, cooperative meeting environment. In six months, I taught these easily learned skills to over one hundred engineers and managers. In follow-up discussions, my former students admitted that they rarely acted as formal facilitators on the job because of time constraints. But they were all pleased with their increased ability to be creative and constructive as *attendees* of meetings.

My experience with zazen practice helped me to recognize the spiritual nature of these ways of being with people. The facilitator's approach is equivalent to maintaining the nonattached attitude of zazen mind. Perhaps Buddhist monks are simply facilitators in disguise, for, as it says in the *Digha Nikaya*, "Thus he is a reconciler of those at variance, and an encourager of those at one, rejoicing in peace, loving it, delighting in it, one who speaks up for peace."[1]

language of the heart

There are certain people we enjoy being with because they speak with complete sincerity, without holding back, willingly sharing both their thoughts and their feelings. We say that these people "speak from the heart." Not only do we enjoy being with them but we admire them for their courage to be open and intimate. But the truth is that when we communicate from a foundation of spiritual practice, we do not require special courage. Our practice itself includes speaking the language of the heart.

Inherently it is not difficult to speak from the heart. But no matter how intelligent or clever we may be, the language of the heart becomes difficult if we forget how to speak it. Zazen practice is the way we remember the language of the heart, the language of the ready mind. This is the language that is not distracted by emotion or critical judgment.

When we study a foreign language, we rely on our intelligence and memory in order to master the vocabulary, grammar, and various everyday expressions of another culture. We make this mental effort so that we can exchange ideas with other people. But the language of the heart is based on our spiritual practice. If we want to communicate openly and sincerely, we do not have to learn a new language. We must simply practice expressing the language we already know, which we have never lost.

At the same time, speaking the language of the heart does not require that we discard the language of the mind. On the contrary, we have to continue using our experience, intelligence, and ability to communicate with each other in everyday life. It is simply a matter of using these faculties appropriately, according to the situation. In our daily lives, we naturally use the capabilities of our thinking and feeling minds. But we should try always to be aware, ready for the next moment. In Zen practice, we do not deny our thoughts and feelings. We just allow the language of the heart to be the source of the language of the mind.

Relationships with each other and with all worldly things are the most important aspect of spiritual practice and of life. If we watch our feelings and emotions, we can tell how we are doing. That is why we emphasize paying attention to the mind and to the way we feel. If we sense that our feelings are not in accord with our true selves, in other words, if we feel out of balance, then we shouldn't follow our feelings, because they do not reflect the language of the heart. It's important for us to let go of these emotions, not be pulled by them, even though at the time we may feel gratified and justified being angry, critical, or impatient.

The appearance of negative feelings in our minds does not mean that we are insincere or inherently bad. It only means that we have some edges that need softening. But we cannot smooth our rough edges with sandpaper. Softening occurs naturally with our understanding of the true nature of things. Ready mind is this understanding; it enables us to let go of our concern for feelings and emotions. We sit down in zazen, expressing our true nature immediately. There is no need to have "perfect" feelings. We simply practice with whatever feelings we have right now. We put our trust in our practice and in our ready minds.

We depend on the language of the mind because we are always working on some practical, everyday problem. We are always involved in situations that are difficult or confusing. But because we must continually rely on our intellects, it is easy to forget the language of the heart. Although the recognition may not be apparent, I believe that everyone who sincerely turns to spiritual practice understands this point in some way. We come to practice because we sense that we have forgotten how to express the language of the heart.

We should know that spiritual life includes the readiness to patiently and wholeheartedly take care of whatever situation we face. Sometimes that includes a problem to be resolved. The best way to solve a problem is through the language of the heart. Naturally we have to use our analytical ability, judgment, and feelings in practical matters, but, the basis for taking care of things in daily life is ready mind. The language of the heart is our natural language. We continue our spiritual practice so that we do not wander away from it.

CHAPTER 11

fearlessness

The devastation that accompanies nature's life-threatening forces—earthquakes, fires, hurricanes, floods, drought—is not the primary cause of humanity's suffering. The primary cause of suffering is the sense of not being loved, of not having been loved, by people who are important to us. This sense leaves us with sadness, grief, for something that is missing. It leaves us afraid.

This fear forms the basis of our human delusions. It creates in us the desire for material and emotional things. The fears of desire manifest themselves relentlessly in our daily affairs. We encounter them at work continually, in ourselves and in others. Most of the time, our response to them is not constructive. The fears associated with career ambitions and the desire for power become the basis for competition, for not being totally forthright, for being at odds with each other, becoming adversaries, even enemies. Politely, we dismiss this unproductive, often destructive behavior as politics, tolerating it as necessary in the business world. But this game creates disharmony and establishes the foundation for stress and more fear.

When we fear the boss who can make or break our career, we don't communicate freely; we hold back and shade meanings by putting a "spin" on the facts, presenting only good news. If we fear being assigned to an undesirable job, or even being laid off, not only do we not trust the boss but we also become suspicious of our fellow workers and compete with them, sometimes undermining them. Not knowing how to respond creatively to fear, we create a war zone.

At work, we find ourselves in the midst of messy interpersonal relationships, continually confronted by unpleasant surprises and setbacks when people do not behave as we expect or need. We spend much of our energy trying to manage affairs and attitudes over which we have little control or influence. Burdened by the fears of desire as the world seems continually to change its mind or erupt in potential disaster, who wouldn't feel anxious, frustrated, and burned out?

But the powerful fears of desire are not inherent. They are the result of the most intangible, most universal anxiety of humanity: the fear that comes from not knowing who we are. The consequence of this fear is a sense of separation from each other and from all things. The real work of our lives is to know who we are, to see beyond unknowing into knowing, past misunderstanding into wisdom, so that we can live authentically, even if circumstances did not, or do not, allow us to be loved as fully as possible.

We can never recover the love that was not given to us in the past, and it does not help to demand that the world love us at this moment. The only antidote for this illness is our own capacity to express love for the world. Known in Buddhism as compassion, this is the ultimate goal of spiritual practice. Practice answers the most important question of our lives: "Who are you before you had an idea of yourself?" Answering this question puts an end to fear.

separation fear: a story

My first experience of separation fear occurred when I was about ten years old. I was overwhelmed by a feeling of loneliness on a muggy Sunday afternoon, one of those New York City summer "dog days" when the air shimmers from the heat, the pavement steams, and automobile hoods are too hot to touch. None of my friends was on the street. On Broadway, there were few people and virtually no traffic. The world seemed ominously still. Sitting on the curb between two parked cars, I was suddenly engulfed by a wave of deep apprehension and sadness. It was a painful, isolating experience, lasting about five minutes. For years, I recalled that feeling, trying to determine its origin. Was it a confused family life? The cruelty of the Second World War, currently under way? An indifferent, impersonal world, embodied by the abrasive New York atmosphere? Eventually I understood that it came from a sense of spiritual separation, from seeing myself as a tiny speck helplessly engulfed by the infinite universe. This experience was the beginning of years of reflection about my life and its relationship to "something bigger."

When we sense the anxiety of separation fear, of not knowing who we are, we are confronted with a choice: we can look directly at it, try to understand it and resolve it, or we can deny and ignore it. The first choice requires determination, the fundamental quality of spiritual practice. The fears of desire dissolve when we overcome the feeling of separation, replacing anxiety and hostility with composure and harmony.

bodhisattva way

The mind clings to ideas about life when it is in constant fear of losing something. And when we do not understand that inherently we have nothing to lose, we cannot recognize or accept our true nature. It is the fearful mind that clings, that cannot be empty. The purpose of zazen is to let the mind be empty, to give the mind a chance to be free from attachment. When we can keep our minds empty moment after moment, we can be free from fear. That is why we emphasize continuing our practice throughout the day.

Buddha's great insight was to appreciate Buddha nature in every person and every creature. He made this discovery when he set aside his mental activity and saw that all beings, all created things, are inherently equal and not separate. Zen spiritual practice and the Zen way of life are based on this understanding.

Everyone, without exception, is a Bodhisattva. But we don't recognize this truth because we have so many ideas about our individual selves. We let our ideas delude us about the true nature of our lives. The Bodhisattva vows emphasize taking care of others, but this taking care is not limited to charity or social action. Our vows include the determination to recognize our inherent Buddha nature. In other words, we vow to accept that we are already Bodhisattvas and to fulfill that role.

I think that secretly we don't want to know about our Bodhisattva nature. Perhaps we feel that it carries too much responsibility. To accept it would mean to stop holding on to self-oriented ideas and to give up desires. We are afraid to give up the pursuit of desires because we think that we won't know what to do instead. We let ourselves become addicted to pursuit, afraid that we will be forever unhappy. However, giving up pursuing and holding on is the manifestation of our vows, freeing us from the limited understanding of our intellects and emotions.

The Bodhisattva does not feel the need to pursue anything. She understands that she already has everything. This understanding expresses itself in practice, so we sit in zazen without expectations. We just sit with awareness and acceptance. To accept that we are Bodhisattvas is our practice. Our greatest joy is to express this understanding in our everyday lives and in each relationship. But we must first have the determination to drop off fear, to understand that we have nothing to lose. Vowing to save all beings means vowing to be who we really are.

giving up self-image

One of the biggest problems we have as human beings is allowing our lives to be consumed by images of ourselves, images that separate us

from others. We have a great tendency to be concerned about the way
we see ourselves and the way we want other people to see us. Because
of our need to feel respected and admired, and our desire to be better than who we think we are and better than who we think others are,
we continually try to develop and protect our self-images, and we constantly compare ourselves with others.

Actually, no one is inherently better than anyone else. Our desire to
appear a certain way is based on a misunderstanding of who we really
are. So if we continually compare ourselves with others, or with some
ideal image of ourselves, we will never be satisfied with our lives. This
effort is like drinking salt water when we are thirsty. It cannot satisfy
our thirst; it will only make us sick.

Even though we may want very much to be "something," actually
we are "not something." During our short lifetime we are "something," unique individuals with our own qualities. Yet in reality we are
nothing special, nothing in particular. We can be who we really are
only by not holding on to images of ourselves.

In zazen, we try to let go of these images; we give up attempting to
be something. So when we practice zazen, we are not limited by ideas
of man, woman, doctor, teacher, student, lawyer, or carpenter. At the
same time, to be "not something" does not mean to be nothing. On
the contrary, it means that we are very big, that we include everything.
It means that we are actually everything. There is nothing outside of
ourselves, so we cannot compare ourselves with anything.

Comparing ourselves with others only encourages our desires to
enhance our self-images, to improve our status in the minds of other
people. It is a mistake to think that we can get somewhere by basing
our lives on judging ourselves and comparing ourselves with others.
The only direction for us is no direction, that is, to have no idea of arriving anywhere and no desire to gain something from our going. If
we desire to gain something by enhancing our images, we limit our
lives and separate ourselves from others. Then we have difficulty living in harmony.

When we are successful at some activity, we may feel proud of what we have done and other people may admire us. But we cannot hold on to the image we think we have gained with our success. It is impossible to "gain" things which are temporary and impermanent anyway by enhancing our images. We are only collecting ideas, stuffing our minds like crowded closets, or attics full of dusty old furniture.

If we try to gain something from our spiritual practice, we will create problems for ourselves and for others. We will dig ourselves into a hole. The more we strive to gain something, the deeper and darker we make our hole and the more discouraged we become. If we use meditation practice to enhance or protect our self-images, even if we practice with great discipline, our practice will be self-oriented.

So we make our best effort to put down the tool that we use to dig our deep hole: the mind that compares itself with others. When we set aside this judging mind, we no longer feel that we are in a deep, dark place. We just feel free. Comparing ourselves with others is not necessary, and it does not help our lives. We should just continue our practice without ideas of differences between ourselves and others.

no limitations

Independent of the skills and capabilities that we may have at any moment, all of us are inherently without limitation. We shouldn't mistake our capabilities and skills for our true selves, which are not limited by the ideas of our small selves. Who we truly are is not dependent on our capacity to do some task at a particular time. When we understand ourselves in this way, we understand that everyone is inherently limitless, and we treat everyone alike, regardless of their skills or capacities. Then we can easily maintain good relationships with ourselves and with each other.

Buddha's spirit of compassion was based on his understanding of the true nature of people. Buddhist compassion is not limited to sympathy or pity for someone in trouble. It is understanding that the human form is finite and that our physical and mental capabilities have limitations. Compassion means that we are ready to help each other express our limitless true selves in the midst of whatever capacities and limitations we have right now. So true helping means encouraging people to express their true nature according to themselves, not according to us. True self is expressed in an infinite number of ways because it has no limits. Each of us has the capacity to express true self in our own unique way. This is an important point in Zen practice.

Usually when we start to practice, we need self-discipline. We have to encourage ourselves to stay on our cushions when we feel discomfort, to return to our cushions when some other activity beckons, or to drop off thinking mind during zazen. Self-discipline is needed when we remain stuck to the notion of limitation and lack of capability. If we think, "I can't do this," we need self-discipline to sit still. Saying, "I can't do this," is the same as saying, "I have a limitation and I will not succeed." But if we have no notion of limitation or of success, we don't need self-discipline. Then practice and life are very natural.

If our legs hurt and our minds are distracted by the pain, our minds have some idea of limitation. But if our minds are not distracted by our painful or sleeping legs, we are practicing without limitation. Even when we have an *idea* of limitation, inherently we are always without limitation.

When the sky is dark at night, the sun is behind us, on the other side of the earth. During the time of darkness, we don't think of looking for the sun. We just enjoy the stars and the night sky. When the sky is cloudy and full of rain, the sun is behind the clouds. At that time also we are not concerned with looking for the sun. We just enjoy the clouds and rain. When the sky is blue, the sun is at one side of us (we cannot see the clear, blue sky if the sun is directly in front of our eyes). In other words, we can only enjoy the blue sky if we do not look directly at the sun. So wherever the sun is shining, we don't think about looking at it. It is not necessary to see the sun directly. We just appreciate the dark sky, or cloudy sky, or blue sky.

When the sun is not in front of our eyes, when we do not see it, it does not mean that the sun has some limitation or that we ourselves have some limitation. If you or someone else lacks some capability, it does not mean that you, or he, is inherently limited. Feeling that way is the result of judging ourselves and others through our thinking minds. When we judge, we develop a feeling of separation by creating ideas of subject and object. Then subject judges object. If we look directly at the sun, our eyes will be blinded. If our minds look only for perfection, they cannot truly see anything. They will always see imperfection and will overlook inherent perfection. We should be like the sun. If we are not shining "here," in this way, we are shining "there," in that way. When the sky is dark, it does not mean that the sun is dark.

Our true selves, our spiritual beings, are inherently unlimited. In our everyday lives, we make an effort to develop our capabilities, to expand the temporary limitations of our form. This is our creative, human effort, how we express our true selves. Making our best effort in the midst of the limits of human form is the way to express inherent limitlessness.

a little bit crazy: a story

"Come down to my office, would you?"

"Be right there," I said.

Apprehension started to rise in my chest as I put down the telephone and prepared to see my boss. You never knew what to expect from him.

I was one of a group of six managers who worked for an extremely intelligent and creative executive. In his years at IBM, he had earned several patents and awards for technical innovation. Normally, he was an upbeat, jolly kind of fellow with an incisive wit. He could be great fun to be around. At times, he was very generous in giving praise and in granting recognition for a job done well.

But he also liked to use his intellect and authority to cajole, manipulate, and threaten. He seemed to take delight in publicly embarrassing people who worked for him. I once watched him bring tears to the eyes of a very competent senior engineer during a meeting with the other managers. Following this meeting, I overheard one of the other managers say to him, "That wasn't very nice." He jokingly responded, "I don't have to be nice when I'm winning." He created uncertainty and stress by giving conflicting instructions and frequently changing plans. He liked to casually mention vague schemes he had in mind for reorganization. Working for him was a challenge.

"Come on in and close the door. Sit down."

I did as he asked, not liking the ominous tone of his voice.

"This memo you wrote, what the hell does *this* mean?"

"Let me see," I said, as I started to get up from my chair. I didn't get far.

"Shut up and sit down!" he shouted.

I was angry and humiliated during the next twenty minutes as we discussed a relatively unimportant item regarding a project I was working on. The memo in question needed only a little clarification; it did not merit the kind of confrontation he was creating. Even though I was aware that my boss sometimes acted a little bit crazy, he had never before confronted me with such anger.

I was in a rage for hours afterward. Early the next morning in zazen, the incident played again and again in my mind. As if watching a movie while sitting on my cushion, I repeatedly saw how quickly I had lost my composure, how instinctively my emotions had taken over.

Weeks later, when my boss confronted me again with his arrogance, I noticed something that had escaped me before. I realized that his irrational anger—demonstrated by his wide eyes, distorted mouth, and tone of voice—was an expression of fear. So even though I felt my own anger start to rise, my awareness of his suffering enabled me to keep my emotions from interfering with the business part of the discussion. By the third time it happened, I did not become upset at his abrasiveness. Recognizing the source of his need to belittle and dominate others, I learned to be patient with his eccentricity and not to take his attacks personally. I made a serious effort to listen, to acknowledge, and not to become defensive when confronted by his verbal digs. After that, our meetings got calmer and more rational. Soon after, he was reassigned as a technical adviser, a nonmanagement position. For the next several years, his innovative and creative abilities led to state-of-the-art solutions to difficult technical problems.

Buddhism teaches that everyone is Buddha but that our easily deluded egos and our fear prevent us from seeing each other in this unlimited way and from treating each other with respect. Zen is the practice of discovering this truth for ourselves, not merely accepting it because it is part of Buddhist scripture. Perceiving each other with the Big Mind of zazen is the same as understanding that there is no need to destroy a relationship when we feel irritated by someone who has acted foolishly or may be a little bit crazy.

the gift of fearlessness

Rational thinking and technology have given our modern world large measures of intellectual and material freedom. But despite its scientific achievements, humanity is still burdened by fear. Our analytical ability and our technology cannot relieve us of deep personal anxieties. In fact, they most likely contribute to anxiety by deemphasizing and diminishing the "irrational," personal element of human relationships. By themselves, they cause us to feel separate from each other and from our world. If we want to overcome these anxieties, we have to resolve feelings of separateness by emphasizing inherent unity. We have to establish stable relationships with each other based on our intrinsic interdependence. Fundamentally, this is a matter of expressing who we really are.

In spiritual practice, we give the gift of fearlessness to each other. In Buddhism, fearlessness is the foundation of spiritual life. Giving fearlessness is equivalent to giving the Dharma, helping people understand the truth. We know that when we have fear and anxiety, our minds are in turmoil and we are filled with confusion. But when we are relieved of fear, our minds can be calm and can let go of delusions and attachments.

If we want to give the gift of fearlessness, we must first have continuous confidence in ourselves. Not just confidence in our capabilities and skills but confidence that comes from understanding our true selves. Then we have to be able to impart this self-confidence to others. We do this through our continual practice, which is the expression of our confidence.

If we have fear, we should not suppress the feeling. We should not try *not* to think about it. Eventually, we will have to face it because we cannot turn away from it indefinitely. If we suppress our fear, we will have to make a continuously greater effort to keep it suppressed; then, when it finally does appear, it will be very strong. Then we will be extremely anxious. We may even explode.

Imagine that we hear a strange scratching, growling noise outside our home and, out of fear, take up a hammer and nail boards across the door. When the noise becomes louder, we nail more boards. With each increase in growling, we nail even more boards so that by trying to keep something out, we nail ourselves in. We have to listen carefully in order to realize that what we hear is not some hungry beast come to devour us. It is just ourselves, wanting to come home. So even if we feel fear, we should try just to sit with a confident attitude. We do not need to wait for fear to subside in order to practice.

We cannot end fear by trying to end it or by keeping it out. We shouldn't try to control our minds or our feelings. Instead, we should stay aware of our fear and attempt to understand its meaning. This

revelation of fear is freedom from it. Fear diminishes when we welcome it.

When we understand ourselves and our own fears, we will be able
to see that our misunderstanding of who we are is the cause of fear.
So when we set aside our egos, we can see the source of other people's fears as well. Then, if they direct criticism or anger at us, we
won't feel it personally. Instead, we will recognize it as an expression
of their own fear and misunderstanding. In that way, we can let our
minds remain stable in the midst of fear and we can give the gift of
fearlessness to everyone.

the wisdom of incompetence

In order to have peace of mind, we must know how to be incompetent. This may sound strange, but actually it is our spiritual practice.
When we start to practice we may think, "Zen meditation will make me
competent." If we practice with that kind of idea, however, we do not
yet understand the spirit of zazen.

Usually, we do not like to feel incompetent. This is because we as-
sociate our feeling of incompetence with a lack of confidence in ourselves. But lack of confidence in ourselves does not come from not
being skilled in some activity or not having complete knowledge
about some area. Lack of confidence arises when we do not recognize our true selves and do not understand the true foundation of
confidence. It means that our view of ourselves is narrow, limited to
our skills and our personalities, to our small selves.

Spiritual practice does not devalue competence. Life is satisfying
when we are competent in many activities. However, life is constantly
changing, and very often we become involved in situations and activities that are unfamiliar to us. We have to work on activities that are
ambiguous and confusing. So we must be ready to act in the midst of
our incompetence.

Our practice is to understand the real basis of confidence. In zazen, we let our minds be as wide as possible, we let them acknowledge and embrace whatever appears. And we take this wide mind into daily life by trying to take care of each thing that appears. Our practice is to take care of what we need to take care of, whether or not we have great skill. We do not worry about being temporarily incompetent. We just place confidence in our true nature and do not worry about small self.

In traditional Buddhist monasteries, monks are given particular assignments. They do not say, "May I have a different job? I am a much better gardener than I am a carpenter." Monks must accept the jobs that are assigned without thinking of competency. We must jump into a job, in total ignorance if necessary. We just jump into it with full confidence. We must be willing to accept incompetence, to go ahead little by little until we know what we are doing.

Unlike the world of business and technology, monastic Zen practice is not concerned with matching highly skilled people to specialized jobs. So, in a way, it is very inefficient. But inherently our lives are inefficient. We are always having to do things we don't know how to do. In terms of efficiency or productivity, that makes no sense, but to express our true nature it is quite necessary.

We need to find ourselves in the big world, the world of our true nature. If we limit our activities to those in which we feel competent, we will limit our lives. We can feel our unlimited lives when we do not intentionally limit our activities. We just make our best effort in all things, big or small. Then our effort includes everything, and we find ourselves in the big world.

Zen practice has nothing to do with judging who "sits well" or who does not. All that is important is that everyone makes his or her sincere, best effort. Whether or not any of us attains something is beside the point. Our continuous best effort in the midst of the world we are in right now is our spiritual practice. To enter enthusiastically into the world of incompetence is enlightenment itself.

To find our lives in the midst of the big world doesn't mean to give up the life of the everyday world. We just do not let our delusions overwhelm us. If we stick only to activities at which we are competent, we are taking care of only a small piece of our minds. But that is not how to have peace of mind. We must give up worrying about pieces of our minds if we are to have peace. Having this kind of attitude, we are never hindered in anything we do or in any relationship.

In zazen practice, strictly speaking, we don't know what we are doing. When our friends ask why we do it, we have no precise answer. We just feel that we must continue. In the midst of uncertainty and incompetence, we express full confidence in our true selves. We know that our lives constantly change and that it is impossible to hold on to comforts we have created for various pieces of our minds. They disappear moment by moment. When we appreciate that truth, we know we must base our confidence on something other than small comforts.

Basing our confidence on our true selves means giving up trying to make pieces of our minds comfortable. In choosing to practice this way, we have given up trading confidence for comfort. So even if we sometimes don't feel so good in our practice, we don't worry. We just put our confidence in our true nature and in our desire to practice.

just something to take care of: a story

My last "career," as a technical writer, began when I had been with IBM for twenty-eight years. It was 1986. The business environment hardly resembled the working world I had entered thirty years earlier. The information revolution had changed the landscape. Gone were the punch cards, the endless turnaround time, and the huge stacks of printed reports. First came on-line video terminals, connected to large mainframe computers, which made information and data processing capability available to individuals in their own offices. Now, personal computers were making it possible to have a flexible work schedule away from the office.

At the time, the company needed writers to provide technical manuals and other documentation for a rising tide of new IBM software products. It was recruiting technical writers from both outside and inside the company. I was on a special assignment in the education area, developing courses to provide new engineering, manufacturing, and management skills to IBM's technical population.

My passion for teaching had been born in the military thirty years earlier, when I taught electronics and radar. I became a very good instructor and, in later years at IBM, developed and taught a variety of classes. Exciting and creative, education was my idea of the perfect job. But the growing field of technical writing offered me a unique opportunity.

I was fifty-three years old, just two years from being eligible for early retirement. In recent years, I had thought about how I could devote more time to Kannon Do and to exploring the relationship of Zen practice to American life. Now technology was offering me the chance. I decided to develop technical writing skills over the next few years at IBM, retire, and, with a personal computer, work as a freelance writer at home, gaining the time and flexibility I needed.

I had much catching up to do at the start of my new career. My writing experience was limited to technical reports, sales proposals, business plans, and interoffice memos; I had virtually no background in writing creatively, in ways that would engage and guide my reader. In addition, my programming skills and knowledge of software were obsolete by at least ten years. Many of the technical writers being hired were young computer science or communications graduates from top universities. Some had Ph.D.'s. From the standpoint of technical competence, I was out of my league. But I was confident that I had enough related experience and background to learn what I needed.

I was assigned to a project that was already under way. On my first day, knowing very little about the new software product or about the tools and techniques of technical writing, I found myself several weeks behind schedule. In midmorning, in the midst of my confusion, a petite young woman walked into my office with a huge armful of documents and manuals. Without pausing to say hello or tell me who she was, she said, "Here's your writer's kit," put the stack on my desk, and turned and walked out. I was startled by her suddenness. I couldn't let her get away; I needed to make as many personal connections as I could in this unfamiliar environment.

Following quickly, I caught up with her halfway down the hall, stopping her long enough for us to introduce ourselves and for me to learn that we were on the same project. She was very bright as well as very shy. She was helpful to me in my early days as a writer.

The first few months were difficult, trying to understand what I was supposed to do, figure out how to do it, and produce some useful work. But I knew that whatever handicaps I had for the moment were just something to take care of. Little by little, I learned the necessary technical skills and became familiar with the new product. At the end of four months, I was no longer behind schedule.

It was hard work but no great accomplishment. People everywhere are continually making this kind of effort because there are times in life when security and comfort need to be placed at risk, when we must be willing to jump into an uncertain situation—one promising a long period of tension and confusion—because we see that something larger is at stake. This was one of those times for me. Thirty years earlier, I am not sure I would have had the necessary determination.

The job of the technical writer includes working with the developers—the programmers—in order to fully understand the functions of the new software product. I had difficulty with one individual, a very bright, energetic young man. I did not understand some of the technical details of the functions his programs were providing, but I had to explain the new functions in the documentation.

The first time we met, he was guarded and reluctant to talk: his answers were incomplete and vague. I had to keep probing to get full explanations. In subsequent meetings, he was impatient with me and with my questions. More than that, he was irritated. Other writers agreed that he was difficult to work with. Yet I sensed that his feelings had nothing to do with us writers. His irritation and impatience—his anger—came from fear.

Sometimes people have difficulty giving, not only giving material things but giving of themselves. They fear that by sharing feelings or ideas—even emotion-free information—they will be giving away their inherent selves, they will "lose" themselves, have nothing to hang on to, and be cast adrift. Their fear expresses itself in anger, with other people and with the world around them. It is no coincidence that in Buddhism *giving* is the first quality cultivated by the Bodhisattva.[1] Overcoming the fear of giving—developing a generous spirit—is the best way to disengage the ego's attachment to itself.

Part of my job was to reduce the tension this programmer felt in working with me. I did not want him to feel that I was taking away something when he gave me technical explanations. Rather, I wanted him to feel that I was giving something, that we were giving to each other. I tried to keep a balanced, unified feeling between us. When I felt a sense of separation developing, I adjusted what I said and how I said it, as well as my gestures, continuously experimenting to find creative ways for us to be together. Whatever I said or did, I tried to leave him with the feeling that "your explanation will help me convey the importance of *your* work to our users." Although our working relationship was never completely easygoing and natural, our meetings became more relaxed, the information exchange more complete.

letting go

no clinging

The Buddhist teaching of emptiness emphasizes the impermanence of all worldly phenomena. It underscores the delusion of mentally holding on to things that have no substantial, permanent essence. We cannot fully appreciate this fundamental truth if we rely only on the words of the scripture; we have to verify it through our own practice. We do so by paying careful attention to the activities of our own minds. By continuously observing the thoughts and feelings that arise, we can recognize that they are transient, that every idea and emotion is very quickly followed by another. The experience of our own meditation practice vividly demonstrates the impermanent nature of all things.

In Zen practice, we make our best effort not to cling to the products of our minds' activity. However, as we soon learn, it is not so easy to let go of ideas and emotions. Our minds are always trying to wrap themselves around "something"—an idea, a fantasy—that they believe, or want, to be tangible. But because this something inherently has no substance, our effort to hold on to it creates confusion and suffering.

Imagine a man who continually keeps his hand clenched in a tight fist. When his friends try to persuade him to let go, he protests that he is holding on to something valuable and that he must keep his hand closed. But when he is encouraged to look carefully at what is in his fist, he sees that he is holding nothing at all. With his mind freed, he can relax his grip naturally.

Feelings and emotions are like smoke; our words, thoughts, and ideas are like clouds. They may be beautiful, and we may like to watch them, but we cannot hold on to them. Unhappiness comes from clinging to beliefs and emotions as if we were children trying to hold on to clouds or bubbles. This is the delusion that Buddhism speaks about. But we should understand that the delusion is in the clinging, not in the belief. By itself, what we believe may be true or it may not, but if we believe in something with clinging minds, there is no room for a new truth or understanding to appear.

Our minds move constantly; we cannot stop them. If we try to stop our minds, we do not understand their nature. Zen practice is to stay aware of our moving minds, to recognize their movement but not be distracted by it. Not being distracted by our moving minds is how we quiet them. So there is no need to try to stop our minds. We just try not to be caught by their movement. Then we can see how things really are.

unclosed doors: a story

"Check these numbers with the financial people."

"You should follow up on that situation."

"Try a different strategy."

"Get Marketing's agreement before you proceed."

"You've got to contact everyone on the list."

I was meeting with a visiting IBM executive. After thirty minutes of this one-way conversation, I was having trouble staying tuned in. Each time he said "should," or in similar language told me what to do, I felt him chipping away at my independence, draining my opportunities to do things my way, to learn for myself. I made note of his suggestions, but mentally I had already closed the door on his ideas.

Reviewing my notes of that meeting a few days later, I was surprised to recognize that his suggestions were valid and useful. The irritating heat of the offending "should" was gone. Time had cooled my emotion. His remarks now appeared in a new light, as helpful ideas instead of attacks on my freedom. It was a vivid illustration of how easily emotions can distort reality.

From then on, I made a point of trying to be aware of feelings that arose during the day. It was not easy. At first, I failed more than I succeeded in noticing my attention starting to fade. But little by little, I learned to sense the flicker of emotions as they began to appear. As awareness increased, I was able to give mental distance to feelings, to separate them from the problem being addressed or the conversation in progress. Stress diminished as hard-edged relationships became smoother and problems easier to resolve.

Over time, distractions tapered off. Mindful attention to both tasks and relationships became natural. Increasingly, I recognized when emotions started to develop and so avoided the stubbornness, criticism, and apathy that they create. This doesn't mean that I achieved 100 percent awareness of every arising emotion. I still became caught in anger, in impatience, in indifference, in a variety of ego-oriented tendencies. But when I recognized what was happening, I had the choice to remain caught by an emotion or to let it go.

Zen practice includes both the awareness and the letting go of desires. The first part is relatively easy. As zazen practice becomes natural, the mind grows soft and flexible, and emotional defenses fall away, revealing our delusions and self-deceptions. After recognition comes the hard part, having the determination not to hold on to the ego's mind games, its discriminations, and its fantasies. This second part—letting go—is the foundation for expressing spiritual practice in daily life. It is based on placing harmonious relations with others ahead of protecting an image of one's self. A photograph of people sitting in zazen may give some idea of what Zen practice looks like. But it is impossible to take a picture of the determination required to put practice into action.

living without regret

Someone once spoke to me about a dying friend of hers who was expressing regret at having so little time left to understand her life. She was concerned about what to say to her friend. It is a touching question and an important one for all of us. I think that the best thing we can do for our friends and loved ones who have this kind of regret is to encourage them to practice awareness in each moment, because understanding of life can only exist in the midst of awareness of our present activity.

If we look back and reflect on what we feel were lost opportunities, we will regret the past. And if we look ahead and feel that we have few opportunities left to us, we will regret the future. But time is not the basis for our lives. Life emphasizes no-time; it emphasizes *now*. So we put our entire lives into the present moment and let the entire world appear in our present activity.

If we regret the harm we created by something we did or said, we can learn from that mistake. It is part of our unfolding wisdom. But we can't dwell on the past; we have to return to the present moment. To have regrets about our entire lives means that we do not understand our lives. It means that we see life encircled by limitations—physical limitations, emotional limitations, and limitations of time. When we let our lives be unlimited, then there is understanding; then there are no regrets, even though we have made mistakes.

As in many other spiritual traditions, in Zen practice we use incense a great deal. We light incense at the start of zazen, and we offer incense during ceremonies. Our lives should be like the incense sticks we offer: both straight and bright. In the darkest room, even one stick of incense provides light. The aroma of incense purifies the room and encourages us. And the ashes of the burning incense falling into the incense vase provide the growing foundation for the next offering.

To offer incense is to offer our lives—to stand upright, to give

light, to purify, and to encourage. In addition, this offering means to
have no regrets as our lives get shorter. We just do our best to burn
as cleanly as we can.

Modern society divides life into various phases. We have childhood, youth, middle age, and old age. Our tendency is to celebrate
youth and regret old age. We regret the so-called passing of youth
because we see life as a series of phases within a block of time. But
actually, all phases exist simultaneously. We can always have the spon-
taneity of childhood, the freedom and curiosity of youth, the creativity and responsibility of midlife, and the wisdom of later years.

The idea of phases in life exists only in the analytical mind. When
we do not see our lives as phases, we are just like incense: we burn
brightly when long and just as brightly when short. Then there are no
regrets.

learning how to work: a story

Hyakujo was one of the most influential Zen masters of the T'ang
dynasty, acknowledged for developing the Zen monastic code and
for establishing an ethic of work and service for Zen monks.
Through his efforts, work became the most significant expression
of Zen practice in daily life.

In his later years, Hyakujo continued to work alongside the
younger monks, cleaning the grounds and caring for the temple
gardens. Concerned that their elderly teacher was working too
hard and knowing that he would not listen to their advice to take
it easy, the monks hid Hyakujo's tools. Without mentioning the
missing tools, Hyakujo immediately stopped eating. Several days
later, becoming alarmed about their teacher's health, they quietly
returned his tools. That day, Hyakujo resumed working and eating
with the monks. In his instruction that evening, he admonished
them that "A day of no work is a day of no food." He died in 814
at the age of 94.

When I first went to Tassajara in 1970, I met many young men and women who were planning to remain at the monastery for several years. I didn't understand why they wanted to stay so long. Why didn't they want to get back to the excitement and challenge of everyday society? I wondered. I asked a man who had been around awhile and seemed to understand what was going on.

"Alan, what are all these young people doing here?"

"They are learning how to work," he said.

It was an illuminating response, whose meaning I understood as I became more involved in the Tassajara routine. On one level, "learning how to work" meant developing the capacity for paying attention. It meant learning how to perform tasks with awareness and focus, without becoming distracted by a yearning to be somewhere else or do something more "exciting," something that promised more personal satisfaction.

Even more, "learning how to work" included "working" within the context of complete spiritual practice that contained many different activities each day. The usual sixteen-hour day at Tassajara began around 5:00 A.M. The physical activity called "work" took about six hours, roughly equivalent to the time spent in the meditation hall for zazen, ceremonies, meals, and lecture. A one-hour study period in the morning, the late-afternoon bath, and personal time after meals made up the rest of the day. "Learning how to work" meant learning that the activity given the name "work" was fundamentally no different than any other activity, each demanding the same complete mindfulness.

My career at IBM was like that, a continuous learning how to work in the midst of changing activities. Over and over, I was a "monk"—a trainee—as a new engineer, a new salesman, a new manager, a new technical writer, each time absorbing new skills and tasks. But even though each new vocation seemed like another phase of my work life, as if something old was ending and something new was beginning, overall there were no phases. It was just one continuous, constantly changing "working" that included many different activities.

Misunderstanding the meaning of work and how to approach it can be a problem for some people. Having learned that I had spent many years with IBM, a young man came to see me to talk about work.

"I'm an administrative assistant for a large software company," he began. "I don't feel it is where I should be or what I should be doing with my life. You've worked for a large corporation for a long time. How do you do it? Do you have any advice?"

He was agitated and clearly unhappy about his present situation.

"What is it that you would rather be doing?" I asked.

"I want to travel and to write. I've done some poetry and I want to write a novel," he said. He gave me a copy of a poem he had written.

"I like this very much," I said. "Have you written many others?"

"No, not so many."

"Why not?"

"Because I have to go to work."

"Why don't you write in the evenings and on weekends?"

There was a long pause, as if he were examining some new discovery. He finally said, in a very quiet voice, "I don't do that."

We talked about the way that Zen practice had helped me understand why work is not limited only to activities that provide an income but rather includes any task we are faced with doing, whether it comes to us by personal choice or through circumstances beyond our control. We discussed how practice enables us to find satisfaction in all activities by learning not to judge them, by not labeling them "good" or "bad," "exciting" or "boring," "work" or "leisure."

Our modern world offers us endless opportunities for creativity, leisure, and earning a living. We can learn how to work in the midst of all these confusing choices—we can take advantage of them and not become distracted by them—when we appreciate that "work" is the expression of our inherent nature, our spiritual practice.

surrender

I once heard a story of a man who went for a hike. While he was walking along a steep path, he slipped and started to tumble down the mountainside. At the last moment, he grabbed a branch that was growing from the side of the mountain. But he could not get a foothold to climb back up. He became frightened. He pleaded: "Lord, please help me! If you get me out of this predicament, I'll do anything you say. Please help me!"

Just then the clouds parted and a voice said, "Did you say you will do anything?"

The man answered, "Yes, Lord, I'll do anything."

And the voice said, "OK, let go."

And the man said, "What! Are you crazy? I'll be killed!"

This story is about stubbornness, about how we refuse to listen to our true selves. Even when we plead with them for help, even when they speak to us directly, we do not listen to our true selves. Instead, we continue to cling to our small minds, which are full of ideas about how life should be. What we really need to do to save our lives is surrender. But it is very difficult for us to relax minds that stubbornly cling to ideas.

When we consider the word *surrender* from a spiritual standpoint, we do not mean it in the usual sense. We do not let ourselves become prisoners. In Zen practice, *surrender* means not "to *give up* our effort" but rather "to *continue* our effort." What we give up is stubbornness, fancy ideas about what we are doing. Surrender actually means understanding that things and ideas have no permanence and that there is really nothing to surrender. When we understand that there is nothing to give up, surrendering is accomplished. Surrender and understanding go together. One does not precede the other.

The story is similar to the well-known Zen parable of a man hanging over a cliff while holding on to a branch with his teeth. Someone comes by and asks him, "Why did Bodhidharma come from the west?" On the one hand, if he fails to answer he will commit a grave sin, because Buddhists make a vow to help people. On the other hand, if he answers, he will fall and be killed. He is faced with a great dilemma.

This story is actually a question about how we want to live our lives. When it was first presented by a Zen teacher, so the legend goes, a monk who was listening jumped up and said, "Don't tell us about the man in the tree. I want to know something about how he got there."

How do we create dilemma in our lives? How do we find ourselves in situations that seem to offer us only bad choices?

Clinging to life with our teeth, with our mouths, is clinging with discriminating mind. Actually, we can't say anything when we cling to life with words. But when we give up clinging to life with our mouths, we can say everything. When we stop clinging with our analytical minds, we understand everything. If we cling, we understand nothing.

We should listen to our spiritual voices. But how can we hear them when our minds are always talking? Our spiritual voices speak in silence. We cannot hear them with our ears. So they are not voices in the usual sense. And, actually, we shouldn't even say "spiritual" as if we were referring to something from another world. Our spiritual voices existed before we had opposing ideas such as "spiritual" and "ordinary," "voice" and "no voice."

When we stop clinging to the branch, we have infinite life. We have unlimited understanding when we let go and do not cling to life with a small mind, the mind of words. We just let go. When we let go, we answer the question "What was Bodhidharma doing?" When we surrender, we are Bodhidharma.

It is not necessary to be concerned with how to take our practice into everyday life. But that doesn't mean we stop paying attention. We just don't worry about "how to." We do not concern ourselves with a plan or technique. We just continue our practice. When our minds return to practice, we are always taking practice into everyday life. Practice means to surrender the small mind, to be empty and ready for anything. Surrender does not mean we give up our everyday lives for something called "spiritual life." To surrender means to give up such distinctions so that there is no difference between "spiritual" and "ordinary." It means to jump into life without distraction.

ocean waves

Most of us enjoy going to the beach. It is a mystical place where the bright, limited, structured world of the land meets the dark, unlimited, flowing world of the ocean. I always feel inspired by the vastness and ceaseless activity of the ocean waves. They appear, disappear, and reappear in new sizes and shapes. Sometimes they seem separate from each other, sometimes they do not. There is a great sense of continuity in their action.

It is the ocean's nature to constantly bring in and constantly take out. The ocean touches the structured land world, then returns to its vast, unlimited world. It reminds us of our original nature, both deep and wide, both coming and going. In the ocean's activity we can appreciate our true selves. Appearing from the vast ocean, the wave is the ocean's activity. The ocean is vastness and the ocean is activity.

Our lives are the same. Our activity takes place in the midst of calmness, in the midst of vastness. However, when we become too busy emphasizing our small, daily activities, we forget about our vastness. We overemphasize the waves of our lives. By forgetting vastness, we try to make our activities seem important.

We have to be careful of creating an idea about our own importance, blowing up our egos as if they were balloons. No matter how big we may want to blow it up, a balloon has limits. But the ocean is limitless, and, in the same way, our true nature is limitless. The best thing for us to do is to give up ideas of the importance of our activities, just letting them appear in the midst of vastness. A wave cannot exist without the ocean, nor can a fish be a fish without the ocean. Our human activity cannot exist separate from vastness. Limitlessness is the source of our limited activities.

To understand the ocean, we have to let our minds be open. We have to enter the ocean of Big Mind. This does not mean that we enter some other world, like Alice stepping through the looking glass. To enter the ocean of Big Mind, we have to feel our limitless selves in the midst of our limited, everyday world. To have Big Mind, we must ourselves be Big Mind. We must be fully aware of our present activity and be determined to care for the present moment.

Like waves, people, things, and activities come and go in our lives. Sometimes we gain something, sometimes we lose something. However, nothing is lost when we continue the ocean of Big Mind. Even if we lose a loved one, there is actually no problem. Naturally we will grieve and there will be sadness. But, fundamentally, there is nowhere to go. There is only the continuation of our original activity.

It is only because we are the ocean that we can have waves. At the same time, because we are the ocean, we must give up individual waves. It is impossible for us not to be the ocean. So we do not emphasize coming and going so much. We just emphasize being the ocean, being truly ourselves.

We cannot express our ocean quality if we are attached to ideas of ourselves. When we are deluded by notions of small self, we forget our true nature. Zazen is how we resume our selfless attitude and express who we really are, how we express the vast, ocean quality of our being.

Even though it is not possible to lose our original nature, it is possible to overlook it. So we practice zazen to express our nature. We cannot be "not Buddha." We are always the ocean. At the same time, we are always the wave. But they are not two worlds. Each activity is the activity of our vast nature.

leaving our caves

Most of us want to see the world only through our own eyes, according to our own viewpoint. But this is like looking at the world from inside a cave. And the farther back we go in our caves, the more narrow our view of the world becomes. We like to stay deep in our caves, surrounded by the dark walls of our old beliefs and opinions. Our caves feel warm and secure. We want to stay out of the cold world of uncertainty, where things constantly change.

We use a variety of weapons, including denial, criticism, and anger, to protect our caves. We use them against others when we feel our caves under siege. But later, if we feel remorse about the bad feelings we created, we have an opportunity to see how we have behaved and how we have been looking at the world. Then we have a chance to see that the world is not just for our own use, that our lives are not just for ourselves. We can see that our own ideas and beliefs are not absolute truth and that there is no need to go to war to protect our caves.

When we have this understanding, we have an opportunity to leave our caves of emotions and beliefs. Then we can see the entire world and things as they are. Zazen practice is how we come out of our primitive caves, how we see in all directions. It is how we let Big Mind appear.

Primitive people took turns guarding caves; soldiers take turns guarding forts and cities; security agents take turns guarding buildings. But no one else is interested in helping us guard our caves. They are our personal caves, and we have to guard them alone. So if we insist on clinging to old beliefs, we must be on guard constantly. But always guarding the caves of our minds limits our lives. Our practice is to give up guarding the small self and feel confident. We let go of the desire to defend ourselves when we understand that there is nothing to guard. Spiritual practice is the way we turn in our weapons.

Letting go of the desire to defend ourselves or guard our caves does not mean that we stop taking care of our lives. Someone once asked, "What does Buddhism say about self-defense?" It is an interesting question. Preserving life is natural, so defending our physical beings does not contradict our spiritual practice. Sometimes we may have to defend ourselves from physical attack. Sometimes our self-defense may be just being careful, such as looking both ways before crossing the street.

But there is also emotional self-defense. If we have stubborn egos, we will want to defend our beliefs and opinions, to guard our caves. When we can let go of our egos, we do not feel a need to defend our ideas against other people. Then we have no denial, criticism, or anger. We just listen and try to understand how they defend themselves. And we see how they suffer and how exhausted they are from defending *their* caves. When we do not engage in emotional self-defense, we do not become bruised and we can help others.

But what do we mean by "self"-defense? What is the "self" that needs defending? Actually, it is very great. We call it Big Self because it includes everything. Big Self is not just me; Big Self is not just you. When we understand Big Self, then we understand self-defense. In its true sense, self-defense is taking care of everything, including each other and our environment. When we have zazen in our daily lives, we can share our practice with everyone. Enlightenment appears when there is neither "us" nor "them." It appears when we completely emerge from the caves of our small selves.

sand castles

Each year on Labor Day weekend one of the beach towns near where we live organizes a sand sculpture contest. People spend many hours creating unique works of art in the sand. The beach is crowded, and everyone has a great time admiring the castles, dragons, trains, cartoon characters, and other artistic expressions. The next day the sand sculptures are gone. The beach is smooth and flat, revealing no trace of what was created.

Inherently, sand is formless. No matter what we do to it, sand re-
tains its fundamental quality. Its very nature is to return to its flat,
smooth, continuous surface. It is always resuming its true nature. Because it is flexible and formless, we can shape sand into any form we
like. But even though we shape it very creatively, sand is always returning to its unbroken, peaceful way. Yet we don't care, because we
know from experience that whatever we create with sand cannot last.
It is because we already know the nature of sand that we can enjoy it.

However, in daily life when we create something that we think is
substantial or permanent, we become unhappy if we lose it. We are
unhappy because we do not understand or do not accept the inherent
insubstantial nature of things. We don't understand that we are still
on the beach. All things have the same nature as sand. Everything is
always resuming its formless, unbroken, peaceful true nature. This is
the only nature things can have. Sand's nature is to run through our
fingers, just as it is the nature of everything to run through our fingers
and to return to formlessness.

The true nature of everything is to express inherent emptiness.
Only in this way can life be ready to accept something new. Whatever
we do with our lives and whatever we create must always be ready for
change. It is the same with ourselves. We are always returning to
emptiness. We are always in the process of giving up form. Otherwise,
life would not be possible. We can live only because we can die.

Emptiness is the source of our existence. We build our lives on
emptiness, and we return our lives to emptiness. We are always coming and going. At the same time, we are not coming, not going. Tomorrow, everything will be gone and everything will be new. Thus
everything is ready again for something to appear.

All things, not only things that look beautiful, are inherently beautiful. If our minds see only the kind of beauty that comes to the eye,
our minds will also see ugliness. Then the mind will think in terms of
good and evil, beautiful and ugly, comfort and discomfort. The mind
will be confused and unhappy. If we see the beauty in something before our minds judge it to be either beautiful or ugly, then our minds

will not think or see ugliness. Seeing beauty before beauty appears to the eye occurs when our minds are empty and are beauty itself. That is how we can understand the true nature of things, which is no different from the nature of sand.

Without relying on the thinking activity of our minds, we can see things as they actually are. To see things only with our minds and eyes is to see life and death, good and evil, beauty and ugliness. To see things without relying only on our thinking minds is to see the true nature of all things on the beach, that is, to see emptiness. Only with the inherent beauty of our empty minds can we build something beautiful, can we create something in harmony with the empty nature of everything.

If we want to live on the beach, we must understand the nature of sand. And we must realize that we cannot change this nature. To misunderstand the nature of sand is to misunderstand ourselves. If we do not truly see the nature of sand, we will live blindly. We cannot control sand because it has its own inherent nature. Our lives are to work and live in harmony with sand and with everything. Then we can create something and discover something. And we can share our creation and discovery with others.

We may remember yesterday's sand sculptures, but we can't touch them. Tomorrow we can go back to the beach and enjoy it. When it is time for something to slip through our hands, we should let it go gladly. This is the only way to have our lives completely.

After four years as a technical writer and almost thirty-two active years at IBM, I retired in 1990. I started work as a freelance writer within a few weeks.

The IBM that I left was far different from what it had been when I arrived. From the very first day, much of my time had been spent in a masculine-oriented culture, frequently characterized by a feet-on-the-desk, shoot-from-the-hip attitude. I loved the excitement of those early days. Over the years, though, that world evolved to a more focused and reflective, less gregarious, less free-wheeling environment.

In many ways, my dual careers paralleled the changes: both had started in "hardware" and finished in "software." In my last "career," I worked with a new generation of highly educated, dedicated, and thoughtful young men and women. We shared a great deal in a short time. I learned new technical skills from them and passed on some of my well-used experience. On my last day, one of the young women gave me a coffee mug. On it was inscribed, "You do everything so well." There was nothing I could say that seemed to fit. We smiled, and then we hugged each other, a gesture that would have raised eyebrows in my "hardware" days. Her sentiment, to whatever extent it was true, was a testimony to how mistakes, confusion, and disappointment can be transformed for the benefit of others.

CHAPTER 13

the spiritual
workplace

If the struggle to survive is the highest priority of living entities—animals, plants, people, and the institutions we create—there is no fundamental reason why it cannot be done with dignity. We want to live with dignity. In the corporate office, on the factory floor, or on the receiving dock, we want our place of work to have dignity and to treat us with dignity. As well as being challenging and rewarding, we want it to be safe and supportive.

But nobody can make that happen for us. A company can establish policies and procedures, and promote a culture that emphasizes respect for the individual, but we can't rely on far-removed executives, or the boss whose office is right next door, to ensure that our personal relationships go smoothly day by day.

The challenge increases as larger companies move away from hierarchical structures and management-dominated decision making. With today's increasing emphasis on customer requirements, interdisciplinary teamwork, partnerships between companies, and decision making at the lowest level, the number of our work relationships is increasing and changing more frequently. The potential for becoming irritated and impatient with each other is rising. Today, along with technical skills, the workplace requires coolness and flexibility.

Other than hermits, few of us have the luxury of avoiding people we would prefer not to work with. So if we want to create and maintain a satisfying, dignified work environment, each of us has to place high priority on maintaining good relationships. Dignity does not mean just looking dignified. Companies as well as individuals can create an appearance of dignity, but to have true dignity wherever we are, each of us must express his or her inherent spiritual dignity.

true sanctuary

When we enter the empty meditation hall, especially for the first time, we experience a tangible awareness of peace. The uncluttered space, accentuated by the orderliness of the simple cushions, seems quietly alive, a reflection of inherent beauty. We find a feeling of safety and of sanctuary.

A large stone church is much like a fortress. With high ceilings and formidable doors, it is a place of refuge and protection. To enter this traditional sanctuary means to enter God's house, the place where we leave the secular world behind, where we are safe from its suffering. In most religious heritages, the sanctuary is off-limits to the secular world.

However, in Buddhism and in Zen practice, true sanctuary is not isolated from everyday life. True sanctuary includes everything, shutting out nothing, because it has no doors and no walls. A true spiritual sanctuary is not limited by a defined space. Nor is it just a place of physical and emotional security. Actually, finding true sanctuary means expressing who we really are. Whatever we may call it—God, Great Spirit, emptiness, the Absolute—true sanctuary is the "place" where we abide in our true selves.

But to abide in our true nature is not so easy because of the stubborn, desirous tendencies of our discriminating minds. We easily forget who we are and so lose our way. We return to our inherent sanctuary—that is, we resume our true nature—through the selfless practice of letting go of mental clutter, letting our minds be wide and spacious.

Tozan and his disciple Sozan were the founders of the Soto Zen school in China. When it came time for Sozan to leave his teacher, he went to say good-bye.

Tozan asked him, "Where are you going?"

"To an unchanging place," Sozan answered.

Tozan then asked, "Is there really any going to that place?"

Sozan responded, "The going itself is unchanging."

In this story, Sozan is saying that the activity is the place of unchanging. He is pointing to continuous effort, uninterrupted practice, as the "place" of sanctuary.

When we experience what zazen practice really is, we can feel true spiritual sanctuary. And we can understand the meaning of our everyday lives and how this meaning can be expressed in each activity, for ourselves and for others. Continuous practice teaches us that each activity is inherently zazen and that sanctuary is realized when we make our best effort to be mindful in all activities. This is our actual practice. It is the only possible sanctuary.

the real priority: a story

Late one Friday afternoon, my final chore before starting the weekend was to update the list of things I needed to do the following Monday. I felt a sense of accomplishment writing my new "to do" list, crumpling the old one, and lofting the paper ball in a high arc, banking it off the far wall into the gray IBM wastebasket. The visibility of the list, the indelible feeling of its individual items, enabled me to avoid the stress associated with my mind's fickle memory. Not only did it protect my sanity but "The List" was an indispensable device for organizing and prioritizing my work.

As it evolved, the list on this particular Friday exhibited an unusual quality, graphically revealing my highest priority: follow-up with the numerous people who had not responded to my requests for information made through calls, correspondence, or personal discussions. The people I worked with, the people I was trying to work with, were not providing the feedback I needed. I had to take the lead to encourage responses, a role familiar to anyone active in the complex business and political worlds of uncertain, changing relationships. I had done it often in the past. This time, however, I was surprised at the extent of my list. Follow-up efforts would take the entire day.

Monday morning I started working my list. The responses were unsatisfying and discouraging.

"What was that you wanted again?"

"Oh, yeah, I'll get to that as soon as I can."

"I passed on your request to Joe; get in touch with him."

"Yes, I gave him the messages you left last week. Do you want to leave another one?"

"Let's see, I think I got your note. It's around here somewhere. I'll check and get back to you."

"Call me again in a couple of weeks."

Toward midday, it was apparent that I was spending too much time on an activity that by itself offered no "value added." It was necessary only because others were slow to respond or had decided not to respond at all. In my frustration, I saw how this behavior was common practice and how often I had done the same sort of thing myself. It made me realize that I did not like being part of a process that was neither productive for the organization nor constructive for myself. What was accepted as a normal part of doing business—ignoring people when we do not feel there is a personal benefit for us in responding—I now saw as placing an undeserved burden on others.

I saw how we allow ourselves to become impersonal in our relationships, justifying our attitude by believing that we must not "waste our time" doing something unnecessary in pursuing our own objectives. Feeling the constant pressure to get things done, to obtain results, we tell ourselves that we need to be "efficient" and "cost effective," and not bother returning calls that do not help us personally.

Organizations and people are successful when they recognize

and take care of important issues in a timely manner and in appropriate sequence. So each of us carries around a list—in writing, in our heads, or in electronic personal organizers, of the things we need to do, and in what priority.

But we create a problem when we think that requests from others are of such little value to us that they *do not get on our lists at all*. We may feel that we have maintained our own efficiency by paying no attention to these requests, but we have actually decreased the efficiency of others, who must wait and then follow up, not knowing if and when their contacts will be acknowledged. We may feel personally efficient, but we have hurt the organization as a whole. More significant, *we have treated others with indifference, without dignity*, creating unnecessary work and frustration for them, and in the long run eroding the community of our workplace.

The futility of following up the items on my list that Monday demonstrated, in a very personal way, the relationship between indifference and the difficulty and delay it creates for other people. In every request for assistance, every overture, every "Good morning"—in all the business, family, or political dimensions of life—I recognized an initiation of a living connection between two people. And I saw that we have to make our best effort to complete that connection, to respond to that overture, if we are to feel our interdependence, the inherent completeness of our lives.

From that day on, I replied to all calls, letters, or in-person questions or requests, without exception. Everything stayed on my list, even though sometimes I had to respond, "I don't know," "I can't help," or "I won't be able to do that until next month." I felt great relief giving up the illusion that taking time to respond to others was somehow inconvenient or that it reduced my efficiency.

How long does it take to respond to someone? A minute? Five minutes? We need only make a small personal investment to show respect for relationships and encourage harmony in our work community. We are shortsighted if we sacrifice this respect to protect our alleged efficiency.

taking for granted

"He took me for granted" was my friend's explanation for breaking up with her boyfriend. Most of us have experienced this feeling, when someone has a casual attitude toward us and gives us little consideration. When we take someone for granted, we feel that we know all there is to know about him, that there is nothing new, and that there is no need to pay much attention to him. We have to be careful of taking things or people for granted, because when we do, we become blind to what and who they really are.

Taking things and people for granted starts with taking ourselves for granted. It happens when we stay comfortable with old assumptions and beliefs about ourselves. We stop paying attention to ourselves and our lives.

Taking things, people, or work for granted leads to carelessness. We forget to take care of family and friends, we overlook the need to take care of our environment, and we neglect to pay attention to what we are doing. By forgetting to take care of ourselves we squander our lives. Spiritual practice is our effort not to take things for granted. Instead, our practice is to see things, people, and activities new in each moment.

When we fall into the trap of taking ourselves for granted, our minds are settled in comfort and we do not make an effort to be aware of what is happening and what is changing in the present moment. At the same time, we have to be careful of not taking our spiritual practice for granted, because it is not fixed; it is dynamic and always changing. Zen practice may look fixed, because its various forms have been used for centuries. Yet even though it follows an established form, it is always ready to change, to acknowledge what is new.

So in our practice we find our way each moment according to circumstances.

Our habit of taking things for granted is based on a misunderstanding of our lives, of seeing things and people as permanent.
When that happens, we may think, "This is the truth," "This doesn't
change," or "This is inherently good and that is inherently bad." Judging things in that way, we cannot recognize that everything is always
changing. Zazen practice is how we understand how to be in the
changing world.

In perhaps his most memorable expression, Zen Master Dogen said:

> To study the Buddha way is to study the self.
> To study the self is to forget the self.
> To forget the self is to be actualized by myriad things.[1]

To study ourselves means that we do not take our own lives for
granted. This is the fundamental attitude of spiritual practice. And to
forget ourselves means that we do not take for granted that somehow,
automatically, we already know everything there is to know about who
we are. In other words, we do not stay stuck with any fixed, unex-
plored ideas about ourselves. Finally, Dogen is saying that we are enlightened by all things when we do not take for granted anything in
this phenomenal world.

If we do not study ourselves and forget ourselves, we fall into the
trap of taking life for granted. This may give us a comfortable feeling, but it is a misunderstanding. Zen practice is nothing but the
continuous study of ourselves and everything we encounter. It is the
way we live a life of awareness, having open, ready minds each moment. If we stop seeing life with ready minds, we will take life for
granted.

In our daily lives, we may obtain things that give us advantages in
our society. We may attain wealth, knowledge, and skills. Most people
work hard to acquire some measure of these things. But if our goal is
to obtain these things for personal reasons only, our lives will be lim-

ited and we will take the gift of life for granted. Advantages are not inherently harmful. It is our attitude toward them that is important. We will have a problem if we are not careful about taking them for granted.

So if we attain these things, we do not discontinue our practice. We continue our effort and our determination to understand and express our lives. That is how we prevent ourselves from becoming selfish with our advantages. We can have great satisfaction when we do not take ourselves for granted. In this way we understand our interdependence and we know how to take care of everything.

Sometimes we meet someone we feel is mean-spirited. Often we have to work with people who rub us the wrong way. How we choose to respond to them determines the satisfaction and peace that we experience in our own lives.

If we meet a difficult person, it is important that we do not take him for granted, writing him off as inherently mean or stupid. We need to understand that he is suffering, that his outer toughness is a sign not of strength but rather of weakness, a defense.

Sometimes we may take someone for granted by doing or saying something harmful. Later, when we recognize that we have damaged the relationship through our own shortsightedness, it is not enough to feel remorse, saying to ourselves, "I shouldn't have said that, but she'll get over it." It is vital to repair the relationship, to eliminate any sense of separation, by apologizing to that person.

Many people feel that apologizing is a sign of weakness and that, in business and politics, it is better to remain more or less "businesslike," even to create adversarial relationships. But that strategy does not work well in personal, family, cultural, or international affairs. It consigns us to our caves. Apologizing is sending a message of acknowledgment that says, "I don't take you for granted; you are important to me." It is an expression not of weakness but of individual strength and of confidence in our relationships with one another. Apology makes the world a safe place to work.

true creativity

To take care of things in the deepest sense is to feel what Buddha felt and to understand what he understood. But if we lose the attitude of taking care, we will lose ourselves and become lost in our lives. If we emphasize taking care only of ourselves, we will not be able to feel the spirit of what we are doing in the world.

We may succeed in obtaining material and emotional things for ourselves. But these things do not last, so we become trapped trying to hold on to slippery, transient things, and to pursue new ones. Despite any success we may have, this kind of life will ultimately feel incomplete. Self-oriented effort is always in vain. In contrast, when we have a spiritual feeling, we understand the true nature of the taking-care attitude. It is simply the Bodhisattva's attitude, the mind of compassion, the mind that spontaneously emphasizes taking care.

Emphasizing taking care doesn't mean that we need to give up our creative activities or stop improving the world around us. It doesn't mean that we have to ignore our inherent intellectual and imaginative powers. The taking-care attitude is a result of understanding the basis for creating something in its truest sense. When we create something—even a word or a look—we should start with a taking-care spirit. Then we can create something that will benefit everyone.

If we have ambitious minds when we go to a monastery for spiritual practice, we will have a problem. We will think: "I am doing good work but nobody compliments me!" Monastic practice emphasizes just taking care of things. That is what is happening day after day. There is no need to worry about being appreciated for our creativity. When we are ready to do whatever has to be done, whether or not the world judges it to be a creative activity, we will be able to take care of things and be creative at the same time.

Buddha was extremely creative. He discovered many truths that escape the busy minds of people. He worked hard to help us recognize and understand these truths. His primary emphasis was discovering the best way to take care of life in this world. That was his everyday activity. We should let our own everyday lives proceed in that way. Then we will find Buddha's enlightenment in each activity. When we let it, enlightenment arises naturally out of daily life practice. Zazen helps us discover and express this kind of mind, which is both the mind that continually takes care and the mind that is always ready to create something.

Creating and taking care are not inherently different kinds of activities. We have no need to distinguish one from the other. We only need to consider them without any discriminating idea. Then we can create whatever we like and we will always have a taking-care attitude.

In the modern world, most people do not like to do maintenance, or what I call taking-care activities. We are materially and emotionally rewarded for artistic activities and for creating things that sell, that are bigger, faster, or more exciting. We are pushed to move on to the next project or activity even before we have fully completed our present project or have cleaned up any mess we have made.

Society sees maintenance as a second-class activity. We have convinced ourselves that when we do that kind of work, we are less important than a person who is creating something new. As a result, we have lost interest in taking care of each other and our world. This is one of the reasons that our school systems are deteriorating. Collectively, we treat schools as if they were institutions simply for taking care of our children, not places for creating, for increasing the wisdom of the next generation and of the entire society. Teachers are treated as if they were doing maintenance, rather than being creative. Our attitude would be different if we recognized that the creative, long-range investment we make in people is far more valuable than the creation of marketable products that will be obsolete in a few years.

My dual careers taught me that sitting on a meditation cushion or in an office, wearing robes or wearing a business suit, are fundamentally not very different. Moving back and forth between formal spiritual practice and the usual activities of everyday life became more and more natural. The workplace became for me a place of fluid relationships rather than an arena of tense confrontations.

My passionate concern for discovering the single, permanent "source" of life evaporated long ago. It was just a feeling, an idea that I once had. Pursuing such a search is as useless as looking for the source of a snowflake. To the strictly analytic mind, the conditions that produce a snowflake—temperature, moisture—do not possess the qualities of snowflakeness. Yet despite what our senses and logic tell us, the unique white crystal appears. The "source" of everything, I discovered, is in the constantly changing present moment.

the river

In Zen practice there is a saying: "To go one step north means to go one step south." It reflects the radical view that in order to go one step forward we have to go one step backward. This paradox was used to challenge Zen monks in ancient China, as in the story of the monk who asked Master Chi-Chen, "What is the way upward?" The master replied, "You will hit it by descending lower."

These puzzling paradoxes are resolved only when we realize that going backward, or south, or lower does not mean retreating. It means simply that we base our daily activities on our true nature. "Going backward" means that we set aside our small, self-oriented minds and resume our original Big Mind.

We misunderstand life if we see it only as a process of going forward. If we think only of going forward, we will be disappointed, because we will never arrive "there." We cannot arrive there because there is no "there," separate from "here." The point is that we have to go back, return to ourselves, ground our activity here. When we are always here, we are always there, and we have no need to worry about advancing.

Modern society requires us to have goals. But if we insist on going forward too fast, we cannot reach our goal. We have to know why we make our effort if we want to reach our goal. In other words, we cannot forget to look back. We have to continually resume our original selves.

Having goals energizes us and helps us create useful things for others. But if we do something only to reach a goal, we will be doing it just for our own sake. On the other hand, if we go back one step each moment, drop off our small minds and resume our true selves, our effort will be made on behalf of everyone.

Life is not a series of incremental advances, a set of discrete steps, like ticks on a clock. If we think it is, we will always worry about our progress and be concerned about self-image. We will lose touch and feel disconnected from our lives. However, if we understand that life is a continuous flow, then we will never lose touch with the source of our lives. Our practice is to continually resume the flow of life. This is how we return to the source, what we mean by "going backward one step."

A life should be like a river, never disconnected from its source. If it is disconnected from its source, there can be no river, because the source is a not static thing. The source is the "flowing" itself. If a river or lake forgets its source, it becomes stagnant and dries up. If we emphasize our small selves, we may make beautiful lakes, but without continuous connection with our flowing sources, we will dry up.

When they return to their sources, the river can flow and the lake can be refreshed. When we return to our true selves, we can be refreshed and our activity can support our lives. Zazen is how we acknowledge our source, the flowing nature of our lives. We are always connected with the source, so we emphasize the flow and say, "Go one step backward."

spiritual life,
daily life

The story of the Sixth Zen Patriarch of seventh-century China describes how an illiterate woodcutter was spontaneously awakened to his spiritual nature when he overheard a reading of the Diamond Sutra. Zen literature is rich with such stories of enlightenment experiences. Not described in these stories, however, is the long preceding period of dedicated, unexciting spiritual practice.

The most important quality of practice is the continual awareness of small, often enigmatic clues that appear throughout life. Waiting passively for enlightenment to display itself in full blossom is like walking through a garden with eyes closed. We fail to see the continuous activity of the universe expressing itself. Practice is the active nurturing of our unfolding spirituality. Spiritual awareness is not diminished simply because we do not experience a sudden insight.

A life based on trying to obtain personal things—emotional, material, or spiritual—can never have enough; it will always feel wanting. There is a limit to what we can obtain. By contrast, if we base our lives on our spiritual nature, we will emphasize our oneness—our fullness—and will never feel lacking. Emphasizing relationships, there is no limit to what we can obtain, no matter what our technical skills or the amount of our wealth.

Emphasizing self-oriented life, our approach to the future becomes "Tomorrow I will get something new." Emphasizing spiritual life, we think instead, "Tomorrow I may meet someone new."

what's the use?

In an informal talk to his disciples, Zen Master Dogen told a story about a discussion he had with a monk when he was in a monastery in China. While Dogen was reading sayings of ancient Zen masters, the monk asked him: "What's the use of reading these Zen sayings?"

Dogen replied: "To understand the actions of the old masters."

The monk asked: "What's the use of this?"

Dogen replied: "I want to be able to guide people when I return to Japan."

The monk asked: "What's the use of all that?"

Dogen replied: "To benefit all beings."

The monk asked: "But what's the use in the long run?"[1]

Dogen reflected on what the monk had said to him. He eventually realized that reading and preaching the sayings of old masters was useless. It wouldn't help his practice and it wouldn't help him guide others. He understood that the monk was right and that he should rely on zazen to provide unlimited ways to guide people. He soon stopped studying the old writings and sayings.

This story tells us a great deal about Dogen's attitude and character. After years of uncertainty and discouragement in Japan, and after a very difficult and dangerous sea journey, he finally arrived in China. At last he was doing what he had been dreaming about, studying the words and sayings of the ancient teachers. Then along came a monk who, by skillful questioning, challenged Dogen's fundamental premise about learning and teaching.

Dogen did not reject what the monk said. Instead, he gave it serious thought. Because he had an open and reflective mind and was willing to listen, he was able to understand that it was a mistake for him to rely on the words of others. This means that he realized that everyone is Buddha, that everyone inherently has wisdom, and that it is useless to recite clever words to people. His encounter with the anonymous monk helped form the foundation of Dogen's teaching, that is, the true way to help people is by encouraging zazen.

Our practice is based on Dogen's understanding that practice is enlightenment itself, that enlightenment already exists within our effort. It means that enlightenment is not the end result of practice and that there are no phases or stages in our practice. Dogen taught that inherently there is nothing to gain. He stressed that great intelligence and skill are not prerequisites for spiritual understanding. Instead, he emphasized the truth of impermanence. He encouraged people to practice with determination and to understand the impermanence of all things. He urged us just to continue making our effort to keep our minds undisturbed, no matter what appears in them.

the best thing that ever happened to me: a story

In the early 1980s, a key engineer and top executive was put in charge of a special quality improvement program in the engineering laboratory at IBM. I was pleased to be asked to work for him; I was interested in the project and liked the fellow. Not only was he very good technically but he was also down-to-earth and pragmatic. He was decisive and knew how to manage projects. In addition, he was good with people; easygoing, generous, a good listener, with a good sense of humor. In short, a real leader.

Working on this program, we got to know each other pretty well. We were not exactly close friends but were comfortable enough so that we could talk about personal matters. As we were walking through the parking lot one day to a meeting, he told me that his father had died when he was very young. He then said, "It was the best thing that ever happened to me."

It was a shattering thing to hear. We walked another few steps; then he added, "I didn't mean that as it sounded." He was fond of his father, he explained, and his father's death had been very painful. "For a long time, I was very unhappy," he said. "I had no enthusiasm for life. Only when I finally stopped feeling sorry for myself about losing my dad was I able to get involved."

Saying that his father's death was the best thing that ever happened to him was his recognition that the difficulties he had faced and resolved as a boy enabled him to appreciate himself and appreciate his life.

impermanence

It often happens that even in the midst of a so-called good life we discover that we feel unhappy or off balance in some way. I think we feel this way when we sense the impermanence and transiency of life but do not fully accept it. Instead, we try to hold on to what cannot be truly possessed. It is like trying to grasp water. We can hold water in the palms of our hands, but we can't close our fingers around it.

Too often, we deny the reality of impermanence and the frightening feelings that accompany it, and continue to act as if it were not true. We refuse to give up what should be given up: our belief in permanence. It is important for us not to deny something that needs to be accepted. Otherwise, our lives and our practice become very difficult. We make our lives difficult by letting our minds be filled with self-oriented ideas and desires that we do not let go.

We experience difficulty in our practice when we continue to act as if impermanence were not true. But our subtle feeling of the reality of this truth remains, so the unhappiness continues in the midst of our denial. True spiritual practice does not require us to change our lives radically. It is simply not fooling ourselves about the reality of the way things are.

original giving mind

When we first begin Zen practice, we may feel that zazen is something we do only for ourselves. So when we reflect on how our sitting practice is going, we may think: "*My* foot hurts," "*My* mind wanders," "*I* get sleepy," "*My* back hurts." Our emphasis is on ourselves because we are concerned about our own physical and mental comfort.

But we misunderstand zazen if we think that it is just a personal practice. We have to be careful not to view zazen as something that we do only when it is convenient or only when we feel comfortable or only when we are in a certain mood. Zazen is not reserved for some optimum moment when we feel "just right." In other words, zazen is not like some commodity that we keep in a drawer or on a shelf for our personal use. The same thing is true about our entire lives.

Our spiritual practice enables us to discover that our lives are gifts to share, not commodities to keep. We also discover that, instinctively, we want these gifts to flow. This is the feeling we have when we practice. Zazen is the way we continually pass on these gifts and the way we let them return.

When we sit down in zazen, we are not limited by our physical bodies. In zazen, we are Buddha's body, the unlimited body. But the unlimited body can only appear when we have gift-giving mind, the mind of Buddha. We have Buddha's unlimited body—Buddha's mind— when we understand our inherent gift-giving nature.

Giving mind appears when we feel gratitude for the gift of life. The nature of our gift-giving minds makes us want to pass on the gift and allow it to continue. The efforts we make based on this gratitude are the expression of our true nature, our original giving mind. We create life each moment with our original giving minds. We let life flow and continue. But if we do not feel our original giving nature the flow is hindered. We become confused, and we create various problems. With original giving mind, we can feel our inherent creativity, which is always fully functioning, even in the smallest of activities.

When people think of death, they usually believe that it means the loss of something personal. One of the greatest causes of human suffering is seeing life and death that way. We cannot feel free if we think that our deaths are personal losses. Freedom means we are always ready to pass on this gift of life, to continue original giving mind.

According to Zen practice, everything *is* Buddha-nature. When we understand this truth, we trust our original nature. We are ready to practice giving because everything is inherently the same.

buddha's footsteps

Zen Master Dogen said that when birds fly in the sky, they leave no trace. And when fish swim in the water, they leave no trace. With this metaphor, Dogen encourages us to understand how to express spirituality in our everyday lives. He is saying that there should be nothing left over from our activity, nothing to clean up.

When we have a feeling of oneness and friendliness with everyone and everything, we naturally want to make our effort to leave no trace. We instinctively want to take care of each other and the house we share. We understand that an attitude of not caring leaves messy traces, creating confusion and a feeling of separation.

Because of the flowing nature of water and air, the gentle traces of the birds' activity and the fish's activity are quickly gone and air and water return to equilibrium. So we say that they leave no trace. But unlike birds or fish, people do not move in the air or in the water. We move on the ground, and we also move in each other's minds. That is the nature of human beings. The ground, the earth, flows more slowly than air and water, so the marks we make in our human world remain a long time. It is the same with people's minds. If we create a trace in someone's mind because of what we say or do, that trace may last for a lifetime. So out of our feeling of compassion, we try not to leave a trace in someone's mind. Birds and fish do not have to make a special effort. They naturally leave their environment undisturbed. But the environment of human activity does not return to balance so easily.

Allowing our minds to be like air or water lets them return quickly to equilibrium and leave no trace of disturbance. When our minds are that way we can notice their tendencies, that is, the times when they do not act like water, when they are stubborn, angry, greedy, or distracted. So we continue our determined practice to let our minds be "no-trace mind." We do this so we will know how to take care of others' minds without leaving a trace.

Our way should be like that of a bird or a fish. We should pass through our environment without a trace of our activity, leaving the earth and the mind undisturbed. Our way is to walk like Buddha. Buddha's footsteps leave no trace, no sound, no mark. When we walk with Buddha's footsteps, we do not disturb anyone or anything with our bodies, speech, or minds.

Along with everyone else who begins to explore formal Zen practice, I discovered very early that this expression of spirituality is relatively easy when we are sitting on our zazen cushions, either at home or in a meditation hall. Alone with our awareness, we feel that we are in a private place. No one is judging our practice, checking our minds to see if they are wandering. The atmosphere is calm, free from the usual daily interruptions and distractions.

We also find that it is not so hard to practice in personal activities, not too difficult to maintain awareness when washing dishes, brushing teeth, rocking the baby, hiking, or eating an apple. These daily tasks provide us an opportunity to appreciate the feeling, the texture, of mindfulness.

But public practice is not so simple. Every one of us continually confronts distractions, from the need to respond to other people as well as from our own sense of responsibility to take care of situations that require attention. Our daily lives are often unpredictable; changes appear suddenly, and our carefully made plans fall apart. How to "go public," to extend what we have discovered in formal meditation practice and in other moments of private mindfulness, has become a large and vital question for the growing number of people trying to understand how to live authentic lives.

For the overwhelming majority, the "real world" of modern society is rough and tumble, emphasizing personal achievement and individuality. Our spiritual practice does not deny these things; it just does not overemphasize them. It discourages promoting ourselves at the expense of others. Instead, it encourages us to free ourselves from the competition of personalities. Spiritual practice emphasizes unity and interdependence rather than separateness. But how do we express our oneness in the world of individuality, where we face abrupt changes, personal competition, judgment, and continuous demands to shift our focus?

There is no simple algorithm or single answer to this question. Each of us has to work it out, find our own way. I have learned that the starting point of this discovery is the trust we place in our inherent spiritual nature and the determination to express it in everything we do.

In my own experience, this determination flourishes out of a sense of inherent unity, a feeling that our lives are not entirely our own, that we are wedded to each other and share the same home. This is an ineluctable sense, like the feeling we have when we walk into a room or garden and smell the perfume of a flower: although we cannot see the flower, its fragrance tells us that it is nearby.

seeing everything completely

The most important point for us is not to limit how we see each other. When we see someone coming down the street and recognize the way she walks, we say, "I know who that is." But do we really know that person? Who is it that we see? When we hear someone's footsteps, we may think we know who is coming. But who do we really hear? To see or hear someone completely is to see and hear with Buddha's eyes and ears.

To see everything completely, we have to open our minds completely. This is like taking off a blindfold that we have had on for many years. Seeing everything completely is the same as coming into the world for the first time, when everything appears fresh and vivid and whole. When we remove a blindfold or come into the world, we see everything all at once. Seeing everything all at once is not the same as simply looking at things. When we develop fondness for some things and discriminate against other things, we limit our seeing and see things only one by one.

To see everything completely is to understand the basis of everything. When we do not look at things with discriminating eyes, we leave nothing out. We see everything equally. When we see in this way, we live completely in the everyday world without being caught by it. And when we see in this way, we actually do not have to say anything. There is nothing to speak of, nothing to think about. This way of seeing is not something to know, it is something to live. It is how we live our lives completely.

To see everything completely we must include everything in our seeing, in the same way that zazen includes everything in awareness. If we want to see things completely, we have to be ready continuously to see anything that appears. We must let go of images that we may have in our minds. If we carry an image in our minds, we will not be able to see fully what we are looking at. And if we carry an image of ourselves, we won't be able to see anything clearly.

To see everything completely we have to return to original darkness. In original darkness, there is nothing in our minds, no images and no shadows. This is the only way to see things as they really are. Original darkness is not the same thing as closing our eyes, putting on a blindfold, or being asleep. Then we cannot see anything.

Original darkness means that we are ready to see everything completely.

Seeing everything completely includes seeing things rationally. For example, if we see steam coming from a pot, we know that the water is boiling or the soup is cooking. If we see smoke coming from the mountain, we know there is a fire. If we see tears, a look of anguish, or a bent posture, we know that someone is suffering. This intellectual capability is a wonderful part of our human nature, but seeing everything completely goes beyond rational seeing. All things in this world can be described by their various characteristics: size, shape, color, sound, function. But the true nature of things is not limited by their physical characteristics. True seeing is letting all things appear as they really are.

We may put limits on our relationship with someone because of how we feel about her individual characteristics or some image of her that we keep in our minds. But when we see everything completely, we can see who she really is. Then our seeing isn't limited by external characteristics and we can establish a true relationship.

When our minds are always ready to see anything that appears, we are awake, we are Buddha. When we see Buddha in everything, in each of us, we see things completely. This is how we let Buddha appear, how we let Buddha function, how we let Buddha see Buddha. This is our way of seeing, this is our practice.

notes

preface

1. Ruth Fuller Sasaki, Yoshitaka Iriya, and Dana Fraser, *Recorded Sayings of Layman P'ang* (New York: Weatherhill, 1971), p. 46.

introduction

1. Shunryu Suzuki, *Zen Mind, Beginner's Mind* (New York: Weatherhill, 1970), p. 133.

1. dual careers

1. J. D. Salinger, *The Catcher in the Rye* (Boston: Little, Brown, 1951), p. 173.
2. The Buddhist equivalent of a saint, an awakened being who sets aside his or her own enlightenment in order to work for everyone's spiritual salvation.
3. Alan Watts, *The Way of Zen* (New York: Pantheon Books, 1957).
4. *Zen Mind, Beginner's Mind* is composed of lectures Suzuki-roshi gave in Los Altos.
5. Katagiri-roshi was Suzuki-roshi's assistant in San Francisco. He later become the spiritual leader of the Minnesota Zen Center in Minneapolis. See Dainin Katagiri, *Returning to Silence* (Boston: Shambhala, 1988).
6. The term *oryooki* refers to the Zen monk's spiritual practice, as well as to the eating bowls themselves. The use of *oryooki* reflects the Buddhist traditions of giving and nonattachment. They have been used in Zen monasteries in China and Japan for over 1,000 years.

3. mind and body

1. Eihei Dogen (1200–1253) was the founder of the Soto school of Zen in Japan. Ignored for several hundred years after his death, Dogen's writings are currently being translated and studied with great interest by both Eastern and Western Zen scholars and practitioners. For a thorough discussion and detailed analysis, see Carl

Bielefeldt, *Dogen's Manuals of Zen Meditation* (Berkeley and Los Angeles: University of California Press, 1988).

5. an adventure

1. Suzuki, *Zen Mind, Beginner's Mind,* pp. 24, 95.
2. For the backgrounds of these three Zen masters, see Rick Fields, *How the Swans Came to the Lake* (Boston: Shambhala, 1986).
3. Marian has written her own story. See Marian Mountain, *The Zen Environment* (New York: William Morrow, 1982).
4. *Haiku Zendo: Chronicles of Haiku Zendo, Including Memories of Shunryu Suzuki-roshi* (Los Altos, CA: Haiku Zendo Foundation, 1973), p. 36.
5. Kobun prefers to be called by his first name, rather than by either of the Japanese Zen honorifics: sensei (teacher) or roshi (master).
6. Eiheiji, literally "Eihei temple," was established in 1243 by Eihei Dogen. It is in the remote mountains of Echizen Province, about three hours by train from Kyoto.
7. Grahame was the first Westerner ordained as a Zen monk by Suzuki-roshi and the first Caucasian to attend a three-month training period at Eiheiji monastery. He was the first president of the San Francisco Zen Center.
8. Literally, someone's wife, such as "your wife" or "his wife."

6. in reality

1. See, for example, Suzuki, *Zen Mind, Beginner's Mind,* pp. 28, 31, and 40.

9. enlightenment at work

1. *Wind Bell* (San Francisco Zen Center), vol. 29, no. 2 (Summer 1995), p. 5.

10. communication

1. Maurice Walshe, *Thus Have I Heard—The Long Discourses of the Buddha* (London: Wisdom Publications, 1987), p. 16.

11. fearlessness
1. The six Bodhisattva "perfections" are Giving, Morality, Patience, Vigor, Meditation, and Wisdom.

13. the spiritual workplace
1. Kazuaki Tanahashi, ed., *Moon in a Dewdrop: Writings of Zen Master Dogen* (San Francisco: North Point Press, 1985), p. 70.

14. spiritual life, daily life
1. Reiho Masunaga, *A Primer of Soto Zen* (Honolulu: East-West Center Press, 1971), p. 34.